Copyright

ISBN (Print): 978-1-7355917-0-4

ISBN (ebook): 978-1-7355917-1-1

Cover design by: Olugbenga Ojuroye

Printed in the United States of America

Dedication

God

Only if I could thank You enough. You're magnificent
beyond imagining

Imoleayo

Titobiloluwa

Tiifeoluwa

Thank you for your support through the years.

You make my life more beautiful than I could ever
imagine.

FINDING
EDEN

The Absolute Truth About
What You Will Experience
When You Start Seeking A
Better Life

OLUGBENGA OJUROYE

Free Audiobook Download

This is to say thank you for downloading the book. Before you read, get your 100% free Audiobook Version of Finding Eden.

Click the link below or copy the link into your browser. https://cloakoffire.com/finding-eden-audiobook-version-100-free/

Book Launch Team

The team who helped spread the word gave this young man a voice in spaces where he couldn't have imagined. God bless you!

Temidayo Afonja

Uzochukwu Nwaogwugwu

Ayodele Ojuroye

Damilola Soetan

Olaitan Ojuroye

Precious Iluku

Modupe Awe

Chinedu Umeh

Laju Dosu

Igado George

Thanks for being a part of this project. God bless you abundantly.

Contents

Foreword

It is always a delight for me as a role model pastor to recognize the next generation of faithful servants God has called to lead the body of Christ. They are not easily recognized, as this present social climate has caused many to remain silent. They observe from the comfort of the pews, looking for affirmation and identifying similarities between their convictions and the inevitable urge to launch out into their calling.

I find myself revisiting the subject of ministry and God's calling from the experiences of my pursuit over the last 37 years. It's never easy, but it needs to be done. What can prepare a Man or Woman to leave the comfort zone of their education and accomplishments and venture deep into the unknown arena of public ministry? How do you embark on a journey guided only by a small inner voice leading you on the path and assuring you that it is okay? You will make mistakes and encounter corrections. Also, you will experience pain and realize disappointments. But, alas! The effort is worth it, and the prize is glorious.

Such a person is the author Olubenga Ojuroye, a humble character and fine gentleman, whom God has touched over his few years in ministry. He is an ardent worshipper. It was clear from our first meeting: Olugbenga is a vessel from whom much is expected, as he is committed to his call and his gift. It is an honor to be tasked with molding part of his life journey.

Finding Eden is a genuine reflection on how a person can ultimately attain right standing with God. It helps you understand the expectation of leading a life of faith while dealing with many challenges as we contend with what we believe is the truth. In this journey, we must all retrace our steps to appreciate the purpose God has placed in our paths. You will contest for every victory before you get any credit.

In the current social climate of media overload and false information, a person has to wonder, how can I navigate the journey of life and end up in Eden, my place of rest? How do I get to the Promised Land God wants me to find and discover?

Be blessed as you allow the dew of wisdom in Olugbenga's revelation and intimate encounters with the Holy Spirit to encourage and challenge you to a deeper walk with God.

Sincerely

Pastor Joshua Shonubi

New Life City Church, USA

Introduction

*The Lord God took the man and put him in
the Garden of Eden to work it and take care
of it.*

Genesis 2:15 (NIV)

Eden is a beautiful place.

Imagine the beauty: the trees, the rivers, and the green
grass. See the never-ending colorful landscape of flowers.
They fill the air with scents that the human mind couldn't
fathom.

Imagine what it would have been like to be in that garden,
God's garden. The large species of wildlife untamed and in
their most excellent glory. The garden is where He needs
us to be. Not bogged down by the trials and difficulties of
life.

Oh! The beauty of dwelling in a home created by God. You
don't have to worry about what's comfortable and what
isn't. You don't have to get confused about the many

selections of furniture. Don't bother about the wall drapes and matching the colors in the kitchen with the living room. There were no buildings back then. So, designing a forest could confuse an interior designer. But imagine being in a place created by the ultimate Gardener and Landscaper—the One whose genes the experts carry. Ever since Eden, men have tried to recapture that environment. But it takes a whole new level of intuition to replicate God!

What about work? Imagine waking up every morning working in a place prepared for you by God? No guessing whether it's your passion or calling. You're not working for the money nor settling for something that's beneath your qualifications. There's fulfillment in work. You go out happy, and you come back home happy, even though there were things you didn't understand or some challenges here and there. Better still, the challenges make you rejoice. And why? Because you know that God is right there in the garden with you to give guidance.

I don't know what you think of when you read God's description of Eden in Genesis, but for me, it is beyond a location. Eden is not only a place that God prepared for our first parents. Eden is an experience. The perfect experience.

Paradise Lost

Then our first parents lost the perfect existence. They lost it! How could they?

It's easy to read about the fall of man and wonder what Adam and Eve were thinking. Yet, God did let us know what Eve was thinking. Since Adam was with her, it's safe to assume he was thinking the same thing.

But haven't we made mistakes that were that dumb? Haven't we all at some point lost something so precious to us over something so valueless and fleeting? Some of us have lost our Eden because our character never measured up. For others, we were not committed to our Eden. We married our Eden but were dating an opposing call. It could be laziness or betrayal that let our Eden slip from our grasps.

You had the perfect job, but you were never able to get to work on time. You found the ideal business but were never able to manage the finances. You married the perfect wife, but for some reason, other women seemed to tickle your fancy. The bottom line, you lost something precious, and you know that your life would be incomplete until you get it back.

There is yet another category of people. These may find it challenging to recognize their Eden. Because, to start with, they never experienced Eden. They are only familiar with peril, confusion, fear, death, and have never known peace. They have never known joy. They can't understand what they missed because they never experienced it. Evil stole life before they ever had a chance to live. The child born into war and has never known a life of peace. The child abused before they could even get to go shopping for a prom dress with their dad. What about the child abandoned on the streets because of a congenital disability? Or the child left because the parents were pregnant out of wedlock?

Some of us have lived hard lives. In some cases, it was of our doing while in others, calamity visited us without an invitation. I'd like you to know that Eden isn't lost forever.

Finding Eden

This book is about helping us navigate the path from where we are to our own Eden. We all know what Eden means to us. Historians have tried to locate Eden for a long time, but no one has found the physical location. However, we are not looking for the biblical Eden. We are looking for our Eden, which may well be different from every other person's definition.

Eden is a place created for us. Be it our piece of real estate, our wives or husbands, our peace of mind. Eden is an experience that describes everything we've ever hoped for or dreamed of in life. A reality tailored for us to enjoy. Some may find our Eden fascinating, while others may find it weird. Not all may agree with the place we get to call home. But for us, without it, we would be like the drowning man who seeks only one thing: air.

Have I found my Eden? It's a difficult question to answer at the beginning of the book. We are on a journey of self-discovery, and it's a question I can't escape. At the end of the book, I'll let you in on my secret.

But for now, let's begin this remarkable journey.

1

His Dwelling Place

Jesus replied, "Anyone who loves me will obey my teaching. My Father will love them, and we will come to them and make our home with them.

John 14:23 (NIV)

Before we talk about where we dwell, let us examine the dwelling place of our Daddy. He determines everything. Finding our Eden will mean nothing if we do not understand where He lives.

The presence of God fascinates man. Man wants to see God. Man wants to be with God. Since God kicked the man from the garden, there has been an emptiness which man has tried to fill. For the most part, this has been one of the primary drives towards idolatry in man.

I have a void that needs filling!

I want to see God!

This quest of man has led him to devise various means and methods to fill the emptiness. Unfortunately, "man" prescribed these methods. God wants us to find Him, so why not ask Him for the way?

The First Idol

> When the people saw that Moses was
> so long in coming down from the
> mountain, they gathered around Aaron
> and said, "Come, make us gods who
> will go before us. As for this fellow
> Moses who brought us up out of
> Egypt, we don't know what has
> happened to him."
> Exodus 32:1 (NIV)

They had dwelt in a foreign land for generations. And in that land, they picked up practices which were peculiar to the Egyptians. The drive of idolatry is the need to observe God with the five senses. Why worship someone or, in their case, something they couldn't see?

They were dependent on their bodies without any spiritual perception of their environment. They also didn't have any direct connection to God. They still looked to Moses as their leader. They saw Moses as the one who brought them out of Egypt and not God. And I understand why they were so wrapped up in Moses and not the God behind the man.

The Egyptians treated their Pharaoh as a god. The Egyptians saw him as divine, and this was the Israelites' culture for 400 years. They lost the experience and concept of an unseen yet powerful God through the ages. The god they could see meant more to them than the God they couldn't see. I dare say that in Moses, they didn't only find a leader; they found Pharaoh's replacement.

When Moses went to meet with God on the mountain for 40 days and nights, they reverted to the way they were on the inside. They built their god, which they could see and attributed to it the mighty works of the one true God. They had hardened hearts. They interacted with God using their heads and not their spirits (Ezekiel 36:26).

I agree the actions of the Israelites were extreme. But Christians still worship idols. Some people look to men as their idols, while other people look at material things in the world as their source. Money and other luxuries have a firm hold on people. But it doesn't fill their emptiness. It doesn't fill the void.

For some, their failure in the quest for God has led them to place themselves as gods unto themselves. They have become masters of themselves—their divine controllers.

But God never wanted it to be that way. God wants to be at the center of who we are because that is where He should be.

Man as a Temple

In the Old Testament, the ark of the covenant signified the presence of God. Anytime they wanted to meet with God, they went to the temple. In the temple, you found God's presence on the earth.

When Solomon dedicated the temple, God said:

> Now my eyes will be open and my ears
> attentive to the prayers offered in this
> place. I have chosen and consecrated
> this temple so that my Name may be
> there forever. My eyes and my heart
> will always be there.
> 2 Chronicles 7:15-16 (NIV)

The temple was for Israel. It was a place where they found the manifest presence of God to handle any situation. This experience was under the old covenant. But what has happened in this new covenant?

God raised Christ from the dead, splitting the curtain in the temple in two from top to bottom. From that time, God moved from that one big house to many little houses that together form one big house.

> Don't you know that you yourselves
> are God's temple and that God's Spirit
> dwells in your midst? If anyone
> destroys God's temple, God will
> destroy that person; for God's temple
> is sacred, and you together are that
> temple.
> 1 Corinthians 3:16-17 (NIV)

> Do you not know that your bodies are
> temples of the Holy Spirit, who is in
> you, whom you have received from
> God? You are not your own;
> 1 Corinthians 6:19 (NIV)

All Christians together form the temple of God. We are temples of the Holy Spirit. God has made His dwelling place with man. So, we can pray anywhere, and God hears us. He dwells in us through His Spirit. His eyes and His heart are right there within us. We don't feel Him with our flesh as the evidence. But His Spirit is right there in us, and we know this by the knowledge of the Bible. That is the proof that He is there.

Give Him an Invitation

Your heart is where God wants to dwell. He desires to be at the center of who you are. But God won't force Himself in. He is not going to break down the doors. Our Lord is a warrior, but He is gentle in certain things. Every house has a door. As the physical temple had a door, our hearts also have doors.

> Here I am! I stand at the door and
> knock. If anyone hears my voice and
> opens the door, I will come in and eat
> with that person, and they with me.
> Revelation 3:20 (NIV)

He knocks until you open. If you don't open the door, He remains outside. But there is something more. It's one thing for God to come into the temple of your heart, but it's another thing for Him to have unrestricted access. For many of us, we've opened the door, but God is not yet Lord. He has access to the living room, but the bedroom is still locked. You still have a safe with so many treasures that you've not disclosed the access codes. God can't open the fridge without you telling Him what He can and cannot eat.

God, don't touch that!

Holy Spirit, what do you want to do with that?

Jesus, that money is mine. I need it to buy the car. Why should I pay the pastor's son's school fees?

Why should I sow this seed?

We've set up motion detectors, alarm systems, and red flags all over the temple. And God can't move to do the great works that He wants to do in our lives.

We desire to sit with Him in heavenly places. We wish to have access to His throne room and all His vast kingdoms on the earth. We want to stand in authority over principalities and powers (Ephesians 1:20-23, 2:6). But how can we have the freedom to rule in His kingdom if He doesn't have the freedom to reign in our temple?

2

Is Your Heart a Home?

As you enter the home, give it your greeting.

Matthew 10:12 (NIV)

In the New Testament, Jesus sent out the disciples in twos. First, He sent the twelve (Luke 9:1-6). Then later, Jesus sent the seventy-two (Luke 10:1-12). When He sent them out, He told them not to take anything material with them: neither food, other sandals, extra clothing, nor staff. They carried no gold, silver, or copper along. Whatever home they went to was to care for all their material needs. They, in turn, proclaimed the good news of the kingdom with signs following.

Are we hospitable to the Holy Spirit?

Does God feel welcome in your heart?

It's one thing for Him to enter and another for Him to relax in You.

It's vital to understand that Eden is nothing without God. Having God move unrestricted in your heart is a significant aspect of your dwelling place.

The first thing Jesus told them to do when they got to a house was to give the house their blessing.

> "When you enter a house, first say,
> 'Peace to this house.'
> Luke 10:5 (NIV)

God will quiet every storm in the house of the person who makes his heart home. It doesn't mean the boisterous winds won't blow, but there is a peace that passes human understanding.

When they found a house that was welcoming, they were to proclaim the kingdom of God. Then heal the sick, raise the dead, cleanse those with leprosy, and drive out demons. They were to freely give to that household what they had freely received (Matthew 10:7-8).

When God comes into your heart and life, He brings His kingdom then He brings His gifts. This thought is a vital point which we will explore later.

Only those who welcome God will get the best of God. Many times, we pray with the impression that God should force us to do the things that are important to Him. God won't pick the lock of your heart. He may knock loudly due to the urgency of His entry, but He'll never break the door down. He does not perform coup d'etat on a person's heart. His love is not forceful, albeit urgent.

Welcome God, Welcome the Blessing

When sending out the twelve, Christ made the following statements:

> "Anyone who welcomes you welcomes
> me, and anyone who welcomes me
> welcomes the one who sent me.
> Whoever welcomes a prophet as a
> prophet will receive a prophet's
> reward, and whoever welcomes a
> righteous person as a righteous person
> will receive a righteous person's
> reward. And if anyone gives even a cup
> of cold water to one of these little ones
> who is my disciple, truly I tell you, that
> person will certainly not lose their
> reward."
> Matthew 10:40-42 (NIV)

Everyone God sends to you carries a reward with him. God never sends anyone empty-handed. God always sends someone to you to deposit something into your life. And in these verses, Christ makes it clear. When He sends a prophet or righteous person to you, they come with a reward. How hospitable are you?

Paul mentioned that some have even entertained angels unawares because they were friendly to strangers (Hebrews 13:2). Paul also said that he longed to visit the Romans that he may impart some spiritual gift in them (Romans 1:11). God's messengers are envoys of His blessing.

When He comes into your heart, it's an opportunity for benefits. He gives you a life-altering experience so that you also can make a dent in the world for Him.

Welcoming the Justice of God

God never fails to bless those who embrace Him. Not welcoming Him only when things are all jolly and gooey. But also welcoming Him when tempted to ask, "Does God really love me?" You cannot choose which side of God you want to live in your heart. The God who prepares a table before you in the presence of your enemies. And the God who comes into your temple to knock down the tables of money changers and foul spirits in your heart. They are one.

Those who are willing to welcome God in His discipline will never fail to receive the best of God.

What Do You Have to Offer?

To be hospitable is to be willing to spend yourself to make another person comfortable. To make them feel at home.

Jesus asked the disciples not to take any supplies but to go to the home of anyone worthy. That person would be responsible for their upkeep until they left the town.

> Stay there, eating and drinking
> whatever they give you, for the worker
> deserves his wages. Do not move
> around from house to house.
> Luke 10:7 (NIV)

God is worthy of an offering. We are to take care of His ministers as they carry out their duties. But one thing is clear from this verse, that everyone has something to offer. Jesus didn't send the disciples to the rich. Their targets were peaceful people. Whatever the person had to offer, they were to receive it. They were not to demand more than the home had to give.

> For if the willingness is there, the gift is
> acceptable according to what one has,
> not according to what one does not
> have.
> 2 Corinthians 8:12 (NIV)

Two stories show how God blessed people for blessing prophets sent to them. These men had nothing material on them to contribute to the household. Still, as the family blessed the prophets, the Lord bestowed blessings on their homes.

The first is the story of Elijah and the widow of Zarephath (1 Kings 17:7-24). God sent Elijah to the woman during a famine. God appointed her to be Elijah's supplier until the end of the season. When Elijah came to her, this conversation took place:

> "As surely as the Lord your God
> lives," she replied, "I don't have any
> bread—only a handful of flour in a jar
> and a little olive oil in a jug. I am
> gathering a few sticks to take home and
> make a meal for myself and my son,
> that we may eat it—and die."
> Elijah said to her, "Don't be afraid. Go
> home and do as you have said. But first
> make a small loaf of bread for me from
> what you have and bring it to me, and

then make something for yourself and
your son. For this is what the Lord, the
God of Israel, says: 'The jar of flour
will not be used up and the jug of oil
will not run dry until the day the Lord
sends rain on the land.'"
She went away and did as Elijah had
told her. So there was food every day
for Elijah and for the woman and her
family.
1 Kings 17:12-15 (NIV).

She had little, but a miracle was waiting for her to give to
the prophet. As she gave, flour didn't run out, and the oil
did not run dry.

During the famine, the widow lost her son (1 Kings 17:17).
And through Elijah, God healed the boy. God acted on her
behalf because of the offering she gave to the ministry of
Elijah. The widow didn't have to borrow to bless him. She
didn't have to steal to provide. She gave of the little she
had, and from then onwards gave back of the blessings that
came into her home.

Elisha and the Shunamite

This story is in 2 Kings 4:8-37. The Shunamite woman had
it on her mind to bless Elisha. At first, she only fed him
anytime he came into town. Then she went on to provide
a room for him in her house. And she continued to be
hospitable towards him. God never chastised the widow
who served Elijah for giving too little. And He never
glorified the Shunamite woman for giving a lot.

Because of her hospitality, God blessed her with a son, even with her husband being old. After some years, the boy died, and through Elisha, God raised him from death.

In both stories, they gave what they had to offer. They both lost their sons after they gave. Yet, because of the presence of the prophets and what they had done, they received their sons from death.

There is an inescapable truth in these stories: Eden requires sacrifice. To find Eden, you must give everything that you have. There is no middle ground. Eden needs an offering.

His Benefits are Never Far Behind

God's benefits always accompany Him when He can reign supreme in the life of His servant.

> Praise the Lord, my soul;
> all my inmost being, praise his holy
> name.
> Praise the Lord, my soul,
> and forget not all his benefits—
> who forgives all your sins
> and heals all your diseases,
> who redeems your life from the pit
> and crowns you with love and
> compassion,
> who satisfies your desires with good
> things
> so that your youth is renewed like the
> eagle's.
> Psalms 103:1-5 (NIV)

The Psalmist yielded his soul and everything to God. As he surrendered, he never forgot any one of the Lord's benefits. This experience is your heritage if you open your heart to God: you are confident in expecting benefits from your Father in all areas of your life.

3

The First Step to Eden

If you will seek God diligently and make your supplication to the Almighty,

Job 8:5 (AMPC)

Every man has a place in God. Every man has an area of assignment. We all have something that God has especially graced us with the wisdom, strength, and power to deliver on. And until we find that place of assignment, we will never find satisfaction in this life. Nothing else will quench our yearning. The question we must ask ourselves in everything we do is: Are we gravitating towards Eden?

No journey begins in God without you seeking Him in earnest. It's easy to wonder, "Why all this fuss about finding Him?" But you see something about God: He longs to infuse us with the best He has to offer. It is not only about the best gifts. But He also wants to give us the best assignments. And assignments always begin with a conversation. The bigger the task, the deeper the conversation.

Think about it. When parents want you to do something small, they give straight forward instructions.

Go get my car keys

Go get the newspaper

But a time comes where it goes beyond instructions. Your parents won't give out instructions like:

Don't marry that woman/man

Be a computer engineer and not an accountant

Such would need much more in-depth conversations than one-liners.

Thus, God would call to reason with us (Isaiah 1:18). The consequences of our assignments are far-reaching in space and in time. God wants you to get your journey right because He knows how important your mission is. It will impact your generation and the generations coming afterward.

Understanding His Plans to Prosper

Whenever God approaches a man, in that first conversation, God always lays out the endgame. He makes it clear what you are going to get out of following and obeying Him.

The first message He gets across to you before you take the first step is this:

> For I know the plans I have for you,"
> declares the Lord, "plans to prosper
> you and not to harm you, plans to give
> you hope and a future.
> Jeremiah 29:11 (NIV)

God would never give you an assignment and take hope away. He will never give you a task that would jeopardize your future because God goes ahead to secure the end from the beginning. He doesn't call you, then starts figuring out what to do with you.

God is good. Many decisions we must make after talking to Him will need us straightening out our lives. Yet He assures us that the end is beautiful.

When He called Abraham, God's first statement made it clear what Abraham was going to get out of the journey.

> The Lord had said to Abram, "Go
> from your country, your people and
> your father's household to the land I
> will show you.
> "I will make you into a great nation,
> and I will bless you;
> I will make your name great,
> and you will be a blessing.
> I will bless those who bless you,
> and whoever curses you I will curse;
> and all peoples on earth
> will be blessed through you."
> Genesis 12:1-3 (NIV)

God made it clear that Abraham's actions will affect his generations. No matter what happened, God made it clear that the end was inevitable if Abraham continued to walk with Him.

When He called Joshua to lead the Israelites, He had a conversation with Joshua. That talk included assurances that the end would be beautiful.

In your quest for Eden, diligently seeking God before you leap would do a couple of things for you.

The first is the assurance of the end. God tells you where you're going to get to and what you will achieve (Joshua 1:2-4).

The second, as He did for Joshua, is that He guarantees your protection. There is no assignment He gives that does not include a risk factor. The devil would always attack and try to abort what God has started. He is crafty, and God gives you His word that He would watch over you even before you take the first step. God told Joshua that no man would be able to withstand him (Joshua 1:5).

Then He guaranteed His presence to Joshua to the end. His presence doesn't mean you won't face challenges. But His presence would always be the game-changer.

These three guarantees serve to cut off fear. God told Joshua not to be fearful but to be courageous. It is what Paul also told Timothy. Should I remind you that every assignment given by God requires boldness? You won't do much if you're scared of everything that happens in the environment.

This fear is the reason for the assurances of God. He gives you guarantees before you encounter obstacles. Because when trying times come, you need something to look back on. You'd need something to hold on to. Because He has assured you, you know you can stand fast in Him. The conditions that are to make you fearful would still be there. Bills and challenging customers would come. The government would make policies that would threaten your journey. But eliminating fear would always get you through.

> For God did not give us a spirit of
> timidity (of cowardice, of craven and
> cringing and fawning fear), but [He has
> given us a spirit] of power and of love
> and of calm and well-balanced mind
> and discipline and self-control.
> 2 Timothy 1:7 (AMPC)

Fear clouds our judgment and doesn't make us think. We cannot reason when we are afraid. We need a well-balanced mind to focus on the goals that God has given us.

Then finally, God makes clear the need to walk in obedience to His laws and commands. God required Joshua and the Israelites to walk the straight and narrow. And that is still a rule in these times as I would later explain.

God Wants You to Find Him

This part is the beauty of the relationship we have with God: He wants you to find Him. He wants to lead and guide you to the place He has prepared for you: Eden.

> Then you will call on me and come and
> pray to me, and I will listen to you.
> You will seek me and find me when
> you seek me with all your heart.

Jeremiah 29:12-13 (NIV)

Come near to God and he will come
near to you. Wash your hands, you
sinners, and purify your hearts, you
double-minded.
James 4:8 (NIV)

Give ear and come to me;
listen, that you may live.
I will make an everlasting covenant
with you,
my faithful love promised to David.
Isaiah 55:3 (NIV)

He needs you to be diligent and focused in your search.
But He is always there waiting. That's why He makes it
clear how to find Him. By purifying your heart and seeking
Him without a doubt. When you do this, He guarantees
that you will find Him. Always.

4

Walking with God Is Rewarding

And without faith it is impossible to please God, because anyone who comes to him must believe that he exists and that he rewards those who earnestly seek him.

Hebrews 11:6 (NIV)

I'd like to emphasize this point about walking with God. If you must call yourself a Christian, then you must be willing to conform to God's way of doing things. Walking with God requires a certain kind of lifestyle if you want to get to your dwelling place.

It's not about what you do when you're in trouble. It's easy to seek God when you know you have no choice. I once saw a video on Twitter that captured the last moments of an airplane that was about to crash. The pilots were able to land the plane with no casualties (thank God!). But it's difficult to believe that many people on a single flight had such close relationships with God. I admit that sounded a bit self-righteous. But in a moment of intense desperation, the lines get blurred. You can't tell who is a believer and who isn't. Crises will cause us to cry out!

People call on God when they are in life or death crises, no matter their faith in life. By instinct, people know that God is the answer. If you know to call Him when in trouble, what stops you from calling Him every other time?

Take a Cue from Enoch

> By faith Enoch was taken from this
> life, so that he did not experience
> death: "He could not be found,
> because God had taken him away." For
> before he was taken, he was
> commended as one who pleased God.
> Hebrews 11:5 (NIV)

Enoch is the only person in the Bible who never experienced physical death. His walk was so close to God that God recalled Enoch to heaven. A factory-recall happens when a product has a flaw that would endanger customers. A message goes out to all customers to send the products back for corrections or a refund.

But Enoch's case was different. God recalled him for functioning too well.

> When Enoch had lived 65 years, he
> became the father of Methuselah. After
> he became the father of Methuselah,
> Enoch walked faithfully with God 300
> years and had other sons and
> daughters. Altogether, Enoch lived a
> total of 365 years. Enoch walked

faithfully with God; then he was no
more, because God took him away.
Genesis 5:21-24 (NIV)

How faithful is your walk? God doesn't need to recall you
to heaven to figure that out. David was a man after God's
heart, but he died a physical death. Abraham was a friend
but still died a physical death. Because God is loving, He
will let you know when your walk isn't straight.

God celebrated Enoch because he was faithful. This
faithfulness is the key to accessing God all the time and
finding your dwelling place in God.

Many times, we make a point of wanting to know God's
will for situations. We find ourselves at critical decision-
making points, and we want to know what God is thinking.
We cry and shout and throw tantrums because God is
supposedly silent. The deadline is coming up! We need
action right now! It's funny how sometimes we are anxious
and apply some level of urgency to situations. Most times,
we don't need the worry only if we were privy to the other
side of our crises!

People of Zion, who live in Jerusalem,
you will weep no more. How gracious
he will be when you cry for help! As
soon as he hears, he will answer you.
Although the Lord gives you the bread
of adversity and the water of affliction,
your teachers will be hidden no more;
with your own eyes you will see them.
Whether you turn to the right or to the
left, your ears will hear a voice behind

you, saying, "This is the way; walk in
it."
Isaiah 30:19-21 (NIV)

It's easier to hear from God from the position of a continuous walk. If you're in the habit of consulting God, the Spirit of God is always right there telling you what to do, even when the decisions are big-ticket items.

Now notice that I said it's easier and not easy to hear from God if you're in the habit of talking to Him. I know it should be easy to speak to a father and for the father to respond or vice versa. But as in father-child relationships, things get in the way.

Sometimes you need to spend hours in prayer or elongated periods fasting and praying. It is not necessarily because of sin. Daniel fasted 21 days before the answer to his prayers got to him. Elijah put his head between his thighs in prayer. Jesus prayed into the night and fasted 40 days. These instances are where the easier clause comes in and not the easy.

Having a continuous walk makes talking to God more natural. And when there is a need to pray 40 days or overnight, the decision comes easier or more naturally. Where the problem comes up is in situations where you are an on-and-off Christian. You may find it challenging to make those kinds of decisions. Even worse, you may find it challenging to recognize the voice of God, let alone understand it.

It is from such people that you will hear statements like, "I'm confused. I'm not sure if this is God or not." If you're not used to hearing from God, how will you understand when He speaks? For such people, the flesh is a significant contender against their spirit. Their flesh is so loud and convincing that they could confuse the loudness for rightness.

Familiarity is vital when communicating with God. Take a husband and wife, for example. With years of experience comes a level of intimacy between them. He knows what she likes to eat, what perfume she wants, and all that. But apart from these superficial things, he knows her body language.

Familiarity with God does not, in any way, mean boring and predictable. God would never cease to amaze me in the way He gets things done. But the closer I get and the more I invest in the relationship, the more I understand His ways. His principles make more sense, and, in that way, I know what to expect.

There are somethings that I know never to think are from God, and there's no confusion. If something happens in my life that doesn't have God's fingerprint on it, I sense that something is off. I'm not always right all the time, though. Like Peter, I also have those moments when God would let down the sheet and say, "take, kill, and eat."

But I'd rather be close to God and stumble as I learn knowing He will support and lift me than to be in a place where a crisis can destroy me because I do not know my Father's voice.

Walking Faithfully

What does walking faithfully even mean? If this is what pleased God about Enoch's life, then shouldn't we get in on it? How faithful could Enoch have been, and how pleasing could he be to God that God decided to take him before death?

I know that's something we may not get to see in our time. Those are not the kind of things you expect to see. If Jesus tarries, everyone has death on their schedule. The best we can do is hope to die old. But to leave this earth without facing death? Things like that only happen on God's terms.

To walk faithfully doesn't mean you won't face death. It does mean that faithfulness is the key to live a life that's pleasing to God. So what does it mean to walk faithfully?

> Now faith is confidence in what we hope for and **assurance about what we do not see**. This is what the ancients were commended for.
> Hebrews 11:1-2 (NIV, emphasis mine).

If you can't believe that God exists without seeing Him, then you can't believe in Him for anything. The verse makes it clear that God commended the ancients for being able to believe in what they could not see. They believed in God without seeing Him.

> And without faith it is impossible to please God, because anyone who comes to him must believe that he exists and that he rewards those who earnestly seek him.
> Hebrews 11:6 (NIV)

We must believe that God exists. You can't please someone dead. It's interesting that in this discourse about faith, Paul takes us back to this foundational truth: God exists. God is real. Even before accepting Christ as Savior, you must believe He exists.

This understanding of God's existence is essential to faith. We can believe because God exists even though we can't see Him. It is the same point that Jesus was passing across to the disciples when He spoke to Thomas.

> Now Thomas (also known as Didymus), one of the Twelve, was not with the disciples when Jesus came. So the other disciples told him, "We have seen the Lord!"
> But he said to them, "Unless I see the nail marks in his hands and put my finger where the nails were, and put my hand into his side, I will not believe."
> A week later his disciples were in the house again, and Thomas was with them. Though the doors were locked, Jesus came and stood among them and said, "Peace be with you!" Then he said to Thomas, "Put your finger here; see my hands. Reach out your hand and put it into my side. Stop doubting and believe."
> Thomas said to him, "My Lord and my God!"
> Then Jesus told him, "Because you have seen me, you have believed; blessed are those who have not seen and yet have believed."
> John 20:24-29 (NIV)

Faith, in its essence, means that your perception does not depend on any of the five senses. In many cases, it's when a man is willing to believe in God when there is evidence to the contrary. Like when Abraham thought he would have a son when there were physical limitations apparent to the eyes and other senses. Or when Mary believed God that she would have a child when she was still a virgin. God commends people who trust Him, not just when there is no evidence supporting that belief, but when every evidence contradicts it.

Rewarding Faith

Now, this is an exciting aspect of faith. The Bible emphasizes the fact that there's nothing we can do to earn things from God. Yet, the presence of the word "rewarder" requires a second look.

Let's do a quick study on this word in the Complete Word Study Bible (CWSB) Dictionary.

Rewarder is the compound word misthapodótēs made up of two words. Misthós, which means reward and apodídōmi meaning to render.

The word misthós generally means wages, hire, or reward as used in this scripture:

> Stay there, eating and drinking
> whatever they give you, for the worker
> deserves his wages. Do not move
> around from house to house.
> Luke 10:7 (NIV)

This passage clearly shows that some aspect of the word has to do with being rewarded for work done. If all good things are by grace, why are we working? Where's the place of diligence? Being diligent indicates a level of thoroughness in the search for something. Diligence is always associated with something you are doing.

Apodídōmi means "To give or to do something necessary **in fulfillment of an obligation or expectation** (CWSB Dictionary, emphasis mine)." God is under an obligation to respond to those who seek Him. An obligation defined not by man but by God Himself. This obligation is because anytime He makes a promise, He swears by Himself.

There are two things we can establish based on this regarding faith.

- Faith involves actions which we can call works, and;
- God put Himself under obligation to respond to our faith actions like an employer of labor.

Now, I understand that this view presents a kind of capitalistic view of God. You must put in the work in this God-child relationship. What about God loving us? What about we being His children? Is there no grace?

Many have mistaken the word grace for something else. But we have preachers coming to the podium to correct this error. The misunderstanding of grace led many people into offense, and even some have renounced Christ.

This line of reasoning is the erroneous thought about grace: we do not need to work for the benefits of salvation.

It sounds like heresy. But that's as clear as I can put it.

5

Whose Work Is It Anyway?

Therefore, my dear friends, as you have always obeyed—not only in my presence, but now much more in my absence—continue to work out your salvation with fear and trembling, for it is God who works in you to will and to act in order to fulfill his good purpose.

Philippians 2:12:13 (NIV)

Salvation is from God. It's a gift that comes out of His love (John 3:16). There's nothing we could do to earn that. No amount of prayer will make you more saved than the next guy. There's nothing like better salvation or levels thereof.

A man believes in his heart and is justified. Then he confesses with his mouth and is saved (Romans 10:10). You can't do any better than that.

After salvation, God gives us that measure of faith (Romans 12:3). We consider ourselves soberly, and we understand that no one is better than the other. At birth, we are all given a clean slate. God doesn't play favorites. For example, Saul and David had equal chances of being great kings. God didn't prefer David to Saul based on something innate.

But our salvation is like the parable of the talents. It's easy to be distracted by how much resources the employer gave each of the workers. However, that shouldn't be the focus. The focus is on what they were able to generate from the resources.

"Well done my good and faithful servant" is not a commendation for salvation. God doesn't congratulate you for being saved. There's a celebration in heaven, no doubt. On earth, there's love and affection and celebration for those who believe openly from altar calls. But there's no commendation.

Think about it. If salvation was the end, then would there be any need to stay on earth after being saved?

With salvation comes a welcome package. In that package, there are tools. You're welcome into a field of laborers plowing a glorious harvest. Every laborer is farming for Eden.

God brings you into a kingdom; you have an assignment with a job description, which is in the Bible. The Bible doesn't just have your job description but also your rewards and benefits.

Now let's get into this mystery of work.

You were Saved to Work

> The Lord God took the man and put
> him in the Garden of Eden to work it
> and take care of it.
> Genesis 2:15 (NIV)

There's work in Eden.

Every believer has a job to do. God saved us, but there are actions we must take on our part to bring out the benefits of that salvation. Some do a better job than others and end up with better results.

The more mature a Christian gets, the more results they produce in the kingdom. The parable of the talents tells a lot about how the kingdom of God works.

> Again, it will be like a man going on a
> journey, who called his servants and
> entrusted his wealth to them. Matthew
> 25:14 (NIV)

What has God entrusted to us? He has assigned the measure of faith (Romans 12:3). That is what God gave us. We received a new life, the Holy Spirit, and faith.

> To one he gave five bags of gold, to
> another two bags, and to another one
> bag, each according to his ability. Then
> he went on his journey.
> Matthew 25:15 (NIV)

He distributed His wealth according to their ability. In the beginning, everyone has a measure of faith. The man who had five bags of gold may not have started with five. There probably was a time he had one sack, and as his ability grew, his employer trusted him with more. The same reasoning goes for the man with two bags and the other with one. Despite the quantity of what they had, one thing they all had in common was that the master gave them resources as a show of trust.

Have you ever thought about the blessings of God being a show of His trust in you? He blessed you with that appointment because He trusts you to multiply it. He blessed you with that marriage because He believes you will treat your spouse and your children right. He blessed you with that ministry because He knows you would work to bring about the best for the kingdom.

On the other hand, have you ever thought about the trials you go through as a show of His trust? What if something contrary to your expectations happens, will you still be a follower of God?

The measure of faith is a needed tool to multiply blessings and stand firm in periods of trials.

He didn't merely give us the measure of faith as you would give a man in need some money by the roadside. No! He entrusted the faith to us. Faith is God's wealth. Faith is the currency of heaven. The more faith you have, the more productive you are.

It is one of the reasons why we should trust God because He first trusted us. The faith we have is a sign of His trust in us.

> The man who had received five bags of
> gold went at once and put his money
> to work and gained five bags more. So

> also, the one with two bags of gold
> gained two more. But the man who
> had received one bag went off, dug a
> hole in the ground and hid his master's
> money.
> "After a long time the master of those
> servants returned and settled accounts
> with them.
> Matthew 25:16-19 (NIV)

Judgment day is not going to be only about how you were able to maintain a sinless life. It goes far beyond sin and punishment. If it was just about sin, then He could just take us up to heaven as we experienced salvation.

The original mandate God gave to man at creation still stands. It cuts through from the Old Testament into the New Testament. Alongside holiness, we are to be productive on the earth. We are to be fruitful, and we are to multiply.

The man who had five bags of gold produced a 100% return. The man with two bags also returned 100%. But the one with one bag returned 0%.

Something is interesting about the commendation the master gave the two productive servants. Did you notice that the master gave them the same praise?

When the man with five gold bags presented his case, this is what the master said:

> "His master replied, 'Well done, good
> and faithful servant! You have been
> faithful with a few things; I will put you

in charge of many things. Come and
share your master's happiness!
Matthew 25:21 (NIV)

When the man with two gold bags presented his case, the
master did not give a different commendation. He did not
give a better tribute to the one who now had ten bags than
the one who now had four. Based on both their abilities
and what the master gave to them, they produced 100%.
They both hit the pass mark.

Remember the story of the widow's mite? Jesus made the
following statement concerning her:

Calling his disciples to him, Jesus said,
"Truly I tell you, this poor widow has
put more into the treasury than all the
others. They all gave out of their
wealth; but she, out of her poverty, put
in everything—all she had to live on."
Mark 12:43-44 (NIV)

She gave more than the rich people because, as a
percentage of what she had, she gave everything. What the
others gave was much and arithmetically more than what
she gave. But she outdid them and got a better
commendation.

Jesus judged her based on two things: her ability and her
willingness to act.

It was where the man with one talent failed. Notice what
the master said after the man had given his explanation.

"His master replied, 'You wicked, lazy
servant! So you knew that I harvest
where I have not sown and gather
where I have not scattered seed? Well
then, you should have put my money
on deposit with the bankers, so that
when I returned I would have received
it back with interest.
Matthew 25:26-27 (NIV)

The first key to his success could have been his ability. He
didn't need to match the output of the men with five and
two gold bags. He didn't have their expertise. God was not
going to judge the man He gave one gold bag based on the
output of the men He gave more. God was going to judge
the one-bag-of-gold man based on his ability.

The second key to his success would have been his
willingness to act. Success only comes after we have taken
a step. The more steps we make, the more His light shines.
That's all this man needed to do. After the man had falsely
judged his master for reaping where he did not sow, the
master revealed the true nature of this servant, which was
laziness.

If you're at work, don't complain if the owner of the
company drives a better car than you or lives a better
lifestyle. Don't complain about you doing all the work and
your boss enjoying the money. You prayed for a job, and
you got it. You saw the job description and the salary, and
you signed the dotted line. Face the task given to you, and
that same owner would reward you.

I'm sure you've guessed by now what the servant with one
bag of gold needed to produce to receive the same
commendation as the man with five sacks.

He needed to produce 100% more than he received. 100% of one is one. All he needed to do was produce one more bag.

As you produce, your capacity to produce more would increase. That's what happened with the man with ten bags of gold. He was given one more bag from the man who didn't produce. If the master were to travel again, he would give ten bags to the man he initially gave five bags and four bags to the man he initially gave two.

We can't become our dreams overnight. But eventually, we can grow into our wealthy place.

Stop All Comparison

The story of these three workers brought a similar parable of Jesus to mind. In Matthew 20:1-16, Jesus talks about a vineyard owner who needed workers to work on his field. He went out early in the morning and hired some workers.

> He agreed to pay them a denarius for
> the day and sent them into his
> vineyard.
> Matthew 20:2 (NIV)

So, the first set of workers started work before daybreak. But the business owner needed more workers, so at various points during the day, he hired more workers to join the first set. Some were even employed an hour before the closing of business for the day. However, when it was time to pay for the work done, he gave all the workers the same wage. The man who worked for 12 hours got equal pay as the man who had been working for 1 hour.

Naturally, there was an outrage from the ones who started work at 6 am. The question is if they were not aware of the other workers' wages, would they have been satisfied with their pay? They wouldn't have been offended. But man's natural disposition is to feel cheated when someone else puts in lesser efforts and achieves either equal or more results.

Another incident took place when Jesus was resurrected from the dead and appeared to His disciples at various times. In John 21, Peter decided he was going back to fishing, and some of the other disciples agreed to go with him. These were men called to be fishers of men. Some would say they had lost hope in their calling, or it wasn't just the same without Jesus being physically present with them all the time. Maybe it was Peter's disappointment in himself for denying Christ that made him think that he couldn't be useful for the kingdom. It was a pivotal moment in Peter's life. Ever since Jesus gave him the invitation to be a fisher of men, Peter never went fishing. Not until now, when he felt like he had failed. I mean, how low can you possibly go from denying the physical Christ? But we all would face challenges like these. Things would happen, be it mistakes initiated by us or attacks from without, that would make us want to give up.

But let's not lose track. Jesus had just finished reproving and reinstalling Peter to his original position when the following conversation took place.

> Very truly I tell you, when you were
> younger you dressed yourself and went
> where you wanted; but when you are
> old you will stretch out your hands,
> and someone else will dress you and
> lead you where you do not want to
> go." Jesus said this to indicate the kind

> of death by which Peter would glorify
> God. Then he said to him, "Follow
> me!"
> Peter turned and saw that the disciple
> whom Jesus loved was following them.
> (This was the one who had leaned back
> against Jesus at the supper and had
> said, "Lord, who is going to betray
> you?") When Peter saw him, he asked,
> "Lord, what about him?"
> Jesus answered, "If I want him to
> remain alive until I return, what is that
> to you? You must follow me."
> John 21:18-22 NIV

Jesus gave an instruction, "follow me." But when Peter saw John, he began to ask Jesus about John. Jesus asked Peter, "What's your business?" Many times, we focus on other people's walk with God. But He wants us focused on what He has called us to do without comparing ourselves with others.

It doesn't matter where you are, compared to others. All you need to do is focus on your calling. It doesn't matter how quickly others achieve their goals compared to you. The main questions you should ask yourself are:

1. Are you giving your vision everything you've got?
2. Are you hardworking?
3. Are you making the necessary sacrifices and moves for your dreams to come true?

How others are doing isn't necessarily a measure of how you are doing because you cannot see 100% of what other people are doing to succeed. You don't know if they should be further ahead of where they currently are. You don't know if they are on schedule. You don't know if they have secret faults God is trying to correct. You probably should be thanking God that you don't have some of the weaknesses that other people have. Everyone would always put their best foot forward on social media. Celebrate with people for their successes, but always remember that you answer to God.

Grace in Your Work

> Therefore, my dear friends, as you have always obeyed—not only in my presence, but now much more in my absence—continue to work out your salvation with fear and trembling, for it is God who works in you to will and to act in order to fulfill his good purpose.
> Philippians 2:12-13 (NIV)

Philippians 2:12-13 starts with the instruction to work out our salvation with fear and trembling. Then goes further to explain that it is God who works in us to do His good pleasure.

What does the Bible mean by the word "work" as used in this verse?

A simple example is when you go to the gym, and someone asks what you're doing. The typical answer would be, "I'm working out." Apart from the food you eat and other things you take in, you're not adding anything new to your body but bringing something out. Your muscles are already there. The abs are already there. Every part of your body is already there. Working out doesn't mean you are sewing muscles unto your body or sticking abs to your stomach.

You're doing exercises to bring something out that already exists.

You have salvation when you believe in your heart, and you confess it. But that's not enough. Can people see your salvation? The whole essence of working out is to produce something visible. It's the process of bringing salvation from the invisible to the visible realm.

To work out as used in verse 12 means to produce. Your salvation is only visible after you take action. If you don't get busy, your salvation remains active only in the spiritual realm.

But as much as it depends on you, it also depends on God. No spiritual work happens outside of God. Look again at the wording of those two verses.

> Therefore, my dear friends, as you have always obeyed—not only in my presence, but now much more in my absence—**continue to work out your salvation with fear and trembling, for it is God who works in you to will and to act** in order to fulfill his good purpose.
> Philippians 2:12-13 (NIV) [emphasis mine].

We are to work out our salvation with fear and trembling "for." In other words, we are to work out our salvation "because" God is working in us on our will and actions. The more we work out our salvation, the more willing we are to do what God wants and the more ability we possess to do what God wants. Nothing happens on this Earth without human intervention.

For God to work, we must be working. When we work from a position of salvation, we allow God to work through us. It is through us that people see the works of God on the earth.

But we need to go a little bit deeper into this thing about work.

Looking again at our scriptures in Philippians 2:12-13, we notice the word "work" appearing twice. The first case is concerning man working, and the second is about God working. The two words do not mean the same thing in Greek.

The first word about man is the Greek word katergázomai, which means to work. This work is what we see. It is "to work by labor or hard work." It's physical—someone typing at his desk, a teacher teaching, or a trader selling. We see katergázomai every day.

The second word, "work" concerning God, is energéō. It is the work God does in us. As can be deduced, this word means to energize or empower. It means what others see is made possible by the work God is continuously doing on the inside.

It is the work of grace inside us. It doesn't matter how we feel on the outside. Sometimes we don't feel like working, and at other times we are so into it that others beg us to stop.

But if God is always at work in us, why do we sometimes struggle to do the tasks He has called us to?

6

How to Access Grace Anytime!

*Let us then approach God's throne of grace
with confidence, so that we may receive mercy
and find grace to help us in our time of need.*

Hebrews 4:16 (NIV)

God has a very distinct open-door policy. He wants you to come as you are, dirty or clean, despite any past wrong decisions or lifestyles. The more unworthy you feel, the more crucial it is that you understand this.

But also, He wants those who are in assignments to come in whenever they need help, strength, wisdom, encouragement, comfort, or they just want to have a break room banter with God.

God wants to talk to His children, and He doesn't want you to be shy about it. He doesn't wish your approach to the throne to be a walk of shame. No matter your condition, He wants you to come to Him with confidence.

God wants you to come to Him like someone who has a right to. He never shuts the door on anyone. On the road to your Eden, you need periodic times of refreshing, and God designed this journey such that the pit stop is always within earshot.

Look at the prodigal son and his father.

> I will set out and go back to my father
> and say to him: Father, I have sinned
> against heaven and against you. I am
> no longer worthy to be called your son;
> make me like one of your hired
> servants.' So he got up and went to his
> father.
> "But while he was still a long way off,
> his father saw him and was filled with
> compassion for him; he ran to his son,
> threw his arms around him and kissed
> him.
> Luke 15:18-20 (NIV)

This young man was about to demote himself to a lower level so that his father could accept him. Jesus made it clear that He no longer calls us servants. God sees humility and responds to it. But for God, humility does not mean demotion to a lesser status than what He sent His Son Jesus to die for.

What would we think of God if, after sinning or making a mistake, the only way He would accept us is if we confess something that is not in agreement with His word? Or would you want to approach a Father who takes you only after He has treated you as an unbeliever?

Notice how the father in this parable ignored the son's apology? The young man was demoting himself to be accepted. But the father would have none of that. He was busy throwing a party and dressing the young man in his sonship attire, which he abandoned when he left home. The father recognized something which was far more important than anything he had to say: repentance.

The sight of his son coming home was more prominent than anything the young man had to say. His repentance was a bigger deal than his apology. They don't always mean the same thing.

No matter what you've done, God never wants to retract your right to call yourself His child. A parent does not disown his child anytime he does something wrong. He corrects and disciplines but never says, "You're no longer my child."

God's door is always open, and He'll never do anything to jeopardize that relationship.

Now, grace is available every time. Whether you feel it at work or not. Or rather, it is most at work when you don't feel it! Let's look at one reason why you can access grace anytime you need it.

God Knows You're Weak Without Him

We must grasp this. Strength as a Christian is not mere bravado or outward toughness. There's more to grace than that.

> For we do not have a high priest who
> is unable to empathize with our

weaknesses, but we have one who has
been tempted in every way, just as we
are —yet he did not sin.
Hebrews 4:15 (NIV)

He's not looking for people to boast in their strength. He's looking for people who will brag about His. That's why with His righteousness, He has also given us free access to His grace. Not only the power not to sin but also not to give up in the face of extreme difficulties or challenges that may come our way.

Notice how the next verse begins with, "Let us then approach God's throne of grace with confidence." We approach God's throne of grace based on what Christ has done and being able to empathize with us. We approach because we are weak and not to prove to God that we are strong. God knows us individually. He knows our nature. The level of insight God has into our lives is so deep. He knows where it's hurting and what we need to do to receive strength.

The next thing we'd notice is the word "confidence." Why should we be confident in approaching God? When you approach your earthly father with confidence, you do so when you pass an exam, win the swim meet, do your chores, or achieve some other feat. You base your confidence on an excellent performance. You hold your head up, and you expect some reward or accolades. As you walk to your father, you smile as you wait for a pat on the back. You've got your good boy swag on.

But imagine you made a mistake. How would you approach your father then? You have your head down and your hands behind your back. As you speak, your father would tell you to speak up several times because he can barely hear you confess. There's no swag, and there's no confidence. If you could blame someone else, you would. This situation reminds us of someone in the Bible.

> Then the man and his wife heard the
> sound of the Lord God as he was
> walking in the garden in the cool of the
> day, and they hid from the Lord God
> among the trees of the garden.
> Genesis 3:8 (NIV)

Adam had no confidence to approach God. He did like some of us do with our earthly fathers. We try to postpone our punishment or discipline. But is this how God wants it? I don't believe so.

God says to come with confidence for two things: mercy and grace. Mercy for when we've done wrong. We come to God for a cleanup. And we are to come boldly to Him and say, "Daddy, I messed up." Even righteous people make mistakes. We are not always perfect as it pertains to holiness or assignments that God gives us to handle. So, we are bold because we expect to get a clean up when we ask for one, not because we are right. Our confidence is in who He is and our expectations of what He has promised to do.

What about grace? Grace has many meanings based on context and translation. According to the CWSB dictionary:

> Grace, particularly that which causes
> joy, pleasure, gratification, favor,
> acceptance, for a kindness granted or
> desired, a benefit, thanks, gratitude. A

favor done without expectation of
return; the absolutely free expression
of the loving kindness of God to men
finding its only motive in the bounty
and benevolence of the Giver;
unearned and unmerited favor.

The definition above is the general meaning, but specific to contexts, we could also find that it means strength, power, healing, gifts of the Spirit, and so much more. But keeping within the meaning of Hebrews 4:15, we would see that grace is a specific response to the weakness identified in man. A fault that Christ empathizes with. Whenever we need strength, the throne room is right there. Just go in there boldly and get some. It's God's righteousness any way, and so we must come in openly using that righteousness.

Accessing Grace

"Ask and it will be given to you; seek
and you will find; knock and the door
will be opened to you. For everyone
who asks receives; the one who seeks
finds; and to the one who knocks, the
door will be opened.
Matthew 7:7-8 (NIV)

How do you access grace? You go to God and ask for it. It's that simple yet so complicated. It's simple to pray for strength when you're in a trial, but I think the complicated aspect of grace is that we do not know when it's working.

The prayer for grace is one of the most biblically accurate requests a person can make. There are tons of scriptures showing that God wants us to have grace. Therefore, in the "will" department, there's no confusion.

But how can it be there, and we do not know it?

Shouldn't it be like eating food? You're hungry and weak, then there's food and water, and you suddenly feel revived. And sometimes it does feel that way. Like Popeye takes spinach and suddenly feels strengthened to take on Brutus.

Then there are those times when it seems so bleak around you, and you're about to give up. You feel you're holding on by a thread that would soon snap. Could grace be at work right in the middle of the most painful experiences of your life, and you're unaware that it's there?

> or because of these surpassingly great revelations. Therefore, in order to keep me from becoming conceited, I was given a thorn in my flesh, a messenger of Satan, to torment me. Three times I pleaded with the Lord to take it away from me. But he said to me, "My grace is sufficient for you, for my power is made perfect in weakness." Therefore I will boast all the more gladly about my weaknesses, so that Christ's power may rest on me. That is why, for Christ's sake, I delight in weaknesses, in insults, in hardships, in persecutions, in difficulties. For when I am weak, then I am strong.
> 2 Corinthians 12:7-10 (NIV)

At this point, Paul was at a low. He was going through many trials and troubles focused on humbling him, but he didn't want the pain. Paul didn't understand why God would allow such to happen to him. But amid the trials, he had a strength that he didn't know about.

While Paul wanted out of the fire and the pain, God was giving him the strength to endure the pain. Paul didn't feel the grace working until God told him it was there. God told Paul that His grace was enough. Could it be that Paul was asking for what God didn't send grace to do? For some, grace means instant healing, while for others, it may involve a doctor's appointment, and for others, it could mean not falling sick at all.

Faith is a means of accessing what grace has made available. We cannot go beyond the grace of God or out-think God's grace. We cannot out-maneuver God. Faith only works if it's in line with the will of God. No matter your level of trust, you can't get more than what the blessing has done.

Paul wanted deliverance, but God's grace wanted humility. While Paul was genuine in his request, he was asking amiss.

But after talking to God, what Paul viewed as the pain became a joy.

When God gives you what is enough, you need nothing more.

But again, is it all determined by our faith? Or, are we saying that grace partial to some? Shouldn't God provide the absolute 100% best outcome all the time? These are questions worth asking.

I feel the need to explore this line of thought further. Two lines of reasoning seem to be against each other. On the one hand, some would see grace as being the absolute best condition.

For example, grace would mean never falling ill or getting healed immediately.

On the other hand, others would see grace as not being in the best conditions all the time. In this case, we trust God to deliver us from the worst of situations, even if they last longer than expected. We experience grace to endure, which eventually results in blessing in deliverance.

For the sick person, grace could mean enduring symptoms, hospital appointments, chemotherapy, and other harsh conditions until healing is physically complete.

Which view is right? Is grace available to keep us from trouble, or is it there to help us through the crisis? Let's explore another bible story to get some perspective on this.

When it Seems Grace is Running Late!

I love the story I'm about to share because it addresses a side of grace that people may diagnose as a lack of faith rather than the discretion of God.

The whole plan of grace is to bring enormous and increasing levels of glory to God in our lives. Faith is what we do on our part to access that grace. Grace seeks out the glory of God, while faith latches on to that grace.

Your faith must hold on to the grace of God as it leads you through the passageways that would get you to experience the glory of God. Christ is an independent thinker and operator. We say His ways are above our ways but do we believe it? Especially when we get stuck in something that is not working out?

On this journey of faith, we need to be mindful of who initiated what. We need to understand who starts troubles, pain, and suffering, and we also need to understand who begins blessing.

I firmly believe that whoever is responsible for initiating the goal is also accountable for the journey that would get you to that goal. Whenever another party who didn't set the destination tries to hijack the process, they won't do an excellent job of the process until the initiator takes over.

Case in point, God initiated the deliverance of the Israelites from Egypt, but Moses tried to hijack the process. He ended up delaying the process by 40 years.

Now let's get on with the beautiful story of Lazarus. There's a lot to learn.

> When he heard this, Jesus said, "This
> sickness will not end in death. No, it is
> for God's glory so that God's Son may
> be glorified through it." Now Jesus
> loved Martha and her sister and
> Lazarus. So when he heard that
> Lazarus was sick, he stayed where he
> was two more days, and then he said to
> his disciples, "Let us go back to Judea."
> John 11:4-7 NIV

Lazarus was sick, and his sisters Mary and Martha had reached out to Jesus. They knew Jesus could heal their brother having healed people many times before.

But, look at the wording of Jesus's statement. This sickness would not end in death but glory.

Even if you pass through death, it would not be the end. It's only a checkpoint on the way. But to get the beauty, they needed grace for death. They needed to endure the bad to experience the good. It means that even when you find yourself in a situation where everything around you is dead, you expect that something life-changing should come after this.

Let's take a closer look at Jesus's motive and action. Jesus loved Mary, Martha, and Lazarus. That's His heart's intention towards them, and us.

Everything Jesus did was because of His love for them.

Then Jesus acted. Instead of going immediately to their aid after hearing the news, He waited two more days where He was. Now, this is interesting. One would naturally interpret a motive such as love by the actions that accompany it. So, on the mere surface of this action, you'll note the contradiction. Was Jesus choosing the glory of God above His love for His three friends?

But how do you interpret a motive like love? When a father disciplines his child, is that not love? When there is a delay in gratification, is that not love? What is faith to do when it encounters a love that demonstrates its essence by delay instead of swift action? Should it give up and say, "this love isn't making me feel good," or should it hold on to that grace and say like Job "Though he slay me, yet will I hope in him" (Job 13:15 NIV)?

Jesus is the one who initiated healing and abundant life. He will bring us through whatever season of death we may encounter on the way to the destination He has for us. And most times, when we face trials, it may seem like He hates us.

Nothing is working! Everything just seems to be going haywire! But of what use is faith if it doesn't hold when everything goes against it? Sometimes we may not know how long our trials would last, but eventually, they'll always come to an end.

Suddenly you'll wake up to a brand-new day. In hindsight, you would meditate and realize that you're better for what you went through even though, at the time, the glory seemed late in coming.

Knowledge Is A Key To Grace

Perspective is a potent thing. There's nothing as beautiful as understanding why we are going through stuff. I can imagine Job being in the throne room when Satan came to ask for some skin.

"God! You allowed that?!"

It would have been a whole new conversation with God, but at least Job would understand. He would know that no one could access him without going through God.

But knowledge about God's will is vital to walking in His grace. Because whatever direction you're going in, learning about who God is and His intentions towards you would get you through or, at the very least, keep you sane. It would help to keep your head straight and focused on an outcome.

Do you know God? Do you understand His ways? What about the immense value that He places on you and the intense love He has for you? I know it could be confusing.

"If He loves me, why would I go through this?"

But understand that because He loves you, He'll preserve you. It helps to look at every experience through the lenses of His love. If you know His love, you can get through anything because God is love, and everything is a product of that love, including grace.

> Who shall separate us from the love of
> Christ? Shall trouble or hardship or
> persecution or famine or nakedness or
> danger or sword? As it is written:
> "For your sake we face death all day
> long;
> We are considered as sheep to be
> slaughtered."
> No, in all these things we are more
> than conquerors through him who
> loved us. For I am convinced that
> neither death nor life, neither angels
> nor demons, neither the present nor
> the future, nor any powers, neither
> height nor depth, nor anything else in
> all creation, will be able to separate us
> from the love of God that is in Christ
> Jesus our Lord. Romans 8:35-39 (NIV)

The love of God is too strong for darkness. The love of God is too powerful for tribulations to overcome you. His love does not mean lack of trouble, hardship, persecution, famine, danger, or sword. These things show up, but grace keeps you stuck on God even through the messy areas of life. Amid the uncertainties of the seasons, some contrasts being as sharp as the difference between summer and winter, accept the truth that His grace is in ample supply.

The knowledge of His love is a powerful key to grace.

Meditation and Confession

My son, pay attention to what I say;
Turn your ear to my words.
Do not let them out of your sight,
Keep them within your heart;
For they are life to those who find
them
And health to one's whole body.
Proverbs 4:20-22 (NIV)

When practiced correctly, these are potent tools in your walk with God. The journey to your Eden is arduous. Some things would happen that would make you want to give up and go home.

But one of the most beneficial things to do for yourself is to internalize the words He speaks to you and go back to them every day. As you meditate and speak those words, they produce life and strength within to carry on. They can transform one's countenance from a sad one to a joyful one, even without anything changing in the environment. That's what meditation and confession are about: internalizing and reminding yourself of the promises of God. In doing this, you create a fire within your heart that lights up the darkness that distractions bring.

In meditation, you draw joy from the future outcome. I remember praying to God for so long about something. When it finally came, it would've been possible to accuse me of being ungrateful. I experienced much joy along the way, meditating and dancing to words that when the outcome was right in front of me, I was like, "Is that all there is?" "Did I overdo the rejoicing?"

Through meditation, you find the grace to experience joy in the wilderness. Although people expect you to be down and out, they see something different about you. It's like a glow. It doesn't mean you don't cry or experience pain. Times would come when you would wonder if God spoke to you. Your mind will attempt to play tricks on you based on the circumstances around you. In meditation, however, we refocus and draw strength from God to plow on towards the expected end despite the outward contradictions.

These are the tools we use to encourage ourselves when filled with fear concerning the vision God placed in us. It's like the story of Jacob in Laban's house when he made massive profits for the business. Let's set the scene.

A young Jacob ran from home to his uncle to escape death at the hands of his brother. He fell in love with his cousin Rachel, but love isn't cheap. He worked for seven years to take her but got duped when in the morning, he found that he had the wrong sister! The young man had to commit to an additional seven years to get the woman of his dreams. Talk about patience and the test of commitment!

After many years of similar experiences where Laban cheated Jacob out of a just reward, he'd had enough. Talk about a toxic work environment! But Jacob had one last idea.

"Laban," he said, "I'm tired of being cheated and not having a fair wage. I have eleven children for crying out loud, and your daughter is expecting! Give me this final contract and keep to your word for a change."

"Alright, son, what do you want?"

"Give me the speckled and spotted cattle among the flock. That way, it would be clear that I'm an honest man, and if you try to cheat me, everyone would know what kind of man you are."

Jacob was in a desperate place. And I'm sure some of us are in situations like these. We are in areas where people continue to take advantage of us, but we can't leave because we don't know what's out there. Or maybe we do know what's out there, but we have the "$100 in hand is better than $1000 outside" mentality. We are afraid that we don't have what it takes to succeed elsewhere.

It could be a job like Jacob's situation. Or maybe it's a relationship where people take advantage of you. You're giving your all, but your innocent heart makes people prone to demand more than they give. You're easy to cheat, but you don't know how to get out of the trap.

But the sad truth about life is that people rarely cheat people mistakenly. When people know they can get away with cheating, they would most likely take advantage of you. And so, Laban did what Laban would do. He called his sons and stole all of Jacob's wages. They took all the speckled and spotted cattle and went on a three-day journey away from Jacob. However, God was watching, and Laban had drawn the last straw.

When Every Condition Negates Your Expectations

There are times when you have hope, but everything around you seems to contradict that hope.

You hope for wealth, but then you lose your job.

You wish for good health, but the doctor gives you a death sentence.

Those vows of forever and ever come crashing when your partner asks for a divorce.

Your child was home-schooled, and you gave everything so that she would have every opportunity you never had. But then you get a phone call from an unknown number, and a familiar voice cries frantically into your ears, "Mama! I'm at the police station!" and your whole world comes crashing.

Your hopes and circumstances have a conversation, but your expectations are weeping while the environment is laughing hysterically. It is a terrible place to be and, perhaps, if you haven't experienced this, I dare say you haven't hoped at all.

This situation is where Jacob found himself after the final deal he made with Laban. He was stuck in a dead contract and was going to walk away with nothing after years of serving faithfully. He was on the clock, and it was time to leave.

But some characters were to play a vital role in helping Jacob recover everything stolen from him: the remainder of Laban's flock.

Everything that was left belonged to Laban and, according to the contract which Jacob continued to honor, Jacob couldn't touch any of them.

The flock couldn't naturally produce speckled and spotted cattle. Jacob had to help them deliver the outcome he desired. He cut out rods such that as the animals looked at them while they mated, it made them produce the speckled and spotted cattle that he wanted. I wouldn't say Jacob genetically modified the DNA of those cattle. But I believe he unlocked an underlying genetic code within the animals.

I dare say that even the cattle producing the speckled and spotted offspring wouldn't recognize them as theirs because they looked so different!

Through meditation and confession of our hope and actions of faith, we unlock the genetic code of the things we require despite what the environment is continually telling us.

Every setback we encounter is pregnant with possibilities. If hope is kept alive, you would soon learn what to do to bring your desired outcome out of the environment.

It is crucial to understand that the environment produces results for everyone. When Laban's cattle went to the water trough and mated, they would have produced offspring. The problem was not that they were barren; they weren't. The problem was that they needed to create for Jacob and not for Laban. Hence, Jacob's dilemma.

Let's look at it this way. The problem is not that people don't want to get married. There's a wedding every weekend, even in a recession. The problem is that nobody wants to marry you. The problem is not that companies aren't hiring. The problem is that out of the million jobs available, no one has called you. There are industries worth trillions of dollars, these industries are liquid in cash and not tied down with assets. Again, the problem is that while other businesses are growing in profit and making money, none of that cash is coming to your business.

The grace we seek is to solve this problem: the move from a place of lack to a place of abundance, the move from the deserted wastelands to our Eden. Keeping the picture in mind by meditation and confession creates a positive environment through which we can get the results we seek. That was the result of Jacob's experiment. He forced the cattle to produce by placing a mental picture before them as they mated, and in the long run, he had more animals than Laban did.

Sometimes it can be difficult, and the negativity around us may seem to overwhelm the dreams within us. But even though hope weeps, it would still produce if it keeps focused. God wants to give you access to the grace that would cause you to create despite the negatives around you.

Aren't You Going to Do Something?

It's interesting how many people get stuck in life because of the unwillingness to act. They have the knowledge, and they've meditated on that for a long time, but in accessing grace, the action is the final step.

I understand that we need to be sure before we act. We've probably made a mistake or two in the past, and these cause inhibitions that prevent us from stepping forward. I know there are a couple of things that would keep us from acting even after much prayer. Let's just lay them out.

The first is the myth of the perfect step. No one ever wants to make a mistake. It's an admirable trait. So, in order not to make "any" mistakes, we compensate by over-preparing. I can bet that many people are still preparing for a move they should have made years ago. I can make a case for the perfect time to act because opportunities come in seasons, hence the phrase "window of opportunity." But an argument for the perfect step? You wouldn't find one because a perfect step requires a perfect man and a perfect man doesn't exist.

Let me burst your bubble. God never calls the perfect person for the job. He calls the person who's willing to do something because perfection comes through doing.

> If you are willing and obedient,
> you will eat the good things of the
> land;
> Isaiah 1:19 (NIV)

Pray all you want, but if you withdraw your hand from the plow when it's time for action, you would have aborted the process that began in prayer.

The second inhibition is the perfect condition. Many people wait for the ideal situation, but the fact is that prayer doesn't always change what you see. In other words, you don't know the effect of some of your prayers until after you've done something.

There were many people in the Bible whom Jesus healed but didn't see the effects of their healing until they took the prescribed actions. He told one to wash in the pool of Siloam, and there he would regain his sight. He said to another to pick up his bed and walk when the leg still looked mangled and weak. The woman with the issue of blood had meditated and concluded that when she touched Jesus's garment, she would get well. What if she met Jesus but turned around and refused to touch His garment?

Another hindrance is that we disagree with God on the action to take. For this, let us look at two examples.

Naaman

The story of Naaman getting well from leprosy is in 2 Kings 5. He was a highly respected commander in the army of the king of Aram. He had achieved victories, but he had leprosy, which was more like a death sentence in those times. People with leprosy were to stay outside the city because they were unclean in the Israelite community.

But he wasn't an Israelite, so his impediment didn't stop him from achieving great things. It's interesting how an obstacle is not a restriction in one community while it is in another. Some people will focus on your weakness and keep you from moving on ahead despite the visible skill sets you possess that are above par.

But his gifts made way for him such that he rose to the level of commander in the army. See how the Bible introduces Naaman:

> Now Naaman was commander of the
> army of the king of Aram. He was a
> great man in the sight of his master
> and highly regarded, because through
> him the Lord had given victory to
> Aram. He was a valiant soldier, but he
> had leprosy.
> 2 Kings 5:1 (NIV)

When you walk with God, don't focus on the "but" circumstances of your life: the lack of the right background, right physical qualities, right skin color, or qualifications that don't match up. Don't despair. Eventually, you will stumble into a circumstance orchestrated by God that would fix your "but."

That was the case with Naaman, who stumbled onto the slave girl owned by his wife. The little slave girl said, "There is a prophet that can heal you." So Naaman packed gifts and went on his way to locate this prophet who could make his problem disappear.

Fast forward in the story to when Naaman arrived at Elisha's house. Now to understand this next part of the narrative, it's essential to understand the context.

Aram was a bigger country than Israel, and tensions were high. The strains were so high that when Naaman presented the letter from his king to the king of Israel, the king of Israel tore his robes! Now Naaman was also highly respected in his own country. So not only was his king great, he was great in his own right.

Imagine his anger when he got to Elisha's house, and the prophet didn't even come out to welcome him. He sent out a servant to deliver the prescription for healing.

> But Naaman went away angry and said,
> "I thought that he would surely come
> out to me and stand and call on the
> name of the Lord his God, wave his
> hand over the spot and cure me of my
> leprosy. Are not Abana and Pharpar,
> the rivers of Damascus, better than all
> the waters of Israel? Couldn't I wash in
> them and be cleansed?" So he turned
> and went off in a rage.
> 2 Kings 5:11-12 (NIV)

Isn't that how we are? God wants to do a mighty thing, but we disagree with God's "how"? We have a better idea than God on how to bless you. For Naaman to get his healing, he had to humble himself and adapt to God's method. His servants even chipped in, saying, "What if God had told you to do something bigger than just simply dipping in the river Jordan?" For some of us, we ought to be glad when God doesn't require too great a thing from us to access Eden. In his humility, he obeyed and realized that the price was not so steep.

Peter

Has God ever told you to do something that contradicts everything you ever knew about Him? Or maybe not everything but some critical aspect that is foundational to your relationship with Him gets opposed by some new tasks He tells you to complete?

That was the case with Peter when God got ready to send him to the Gentiles. God had met with Cornelius and told him to send men to Joppa to look for Peter. Again, the political climate didn't encourage this at the time. There was no interaction between Jews and Gentiles. They didn't worship the same God. God Himself had forbidden the Israelites from interacting with the Gentiles lest they become corrupted and unclean. So, imagine Peter's dilemma when the sheet came down from heaven telling him to kill an unclean animal and eat it. You could hear the wonder in his response.

> "Surely not, Lord!" Peter replied. "I
> have never eaten anything impure or
> unclean."
> Acts 10:14 (NIV)

The first thing to notice is that Peter didn't attribute the vision to the devil. The instruction contradicted God's ruling as regards eating unclean things. But, taking a cue from Jesus, you would notice that the foundation of that rule was beginning to shatter when Jesus healed the Syrophoenician woman's daughter and conversed with the Samaritan woman at the well. So, Peter didn't respond to the voice with "get thee behind me, Satan." He replied, "Surely not, Lord." He knew who was talking to him because the relationship was there.

Be ready! On the journey to Eden, God would expect you to change some things even though they supposedly contradict a previous instruction.

Another significant thing is that God spoke to Peter as He would have talked to Peter in previous times. He recognized God. Peter knew the same voice that instructed him to speak on the day of Pentecost and to heal the disabled man at the gate of the temple. He did not disregard the familiar voice of his Lord because of an unfamiliar command.

To access grace for complicated things, we must accept that God tells us to do unpopular things. God still gives us instructions that require us to humble ourselves. We will never see the fullness of God's grace if we pick and choose which commands we obey. And I dare say that the greater glory comes from actions that require greater humility.

Another thing to notice is that God does not reveal everything all at once. It was His plan right from the beginning to include the Gentiles in the scheme of salvation. Revelation is indeed progressive, and we act based on the revelation for that season.

Peter went ahead to Cornelius, and before he could get to the meat of his speech, the Holy Spirit fell on Cornelius and his household. You could even say that God just wanted Peter there as a witness rather than an instrument to cause the Holy Spirit to descend on the people.

That is how the grace of God is released. When we act on His instructions, everything begins to fall into place. Like Naaman, we have to eliminate my pride. Like Peter, we have to go ahead to act, even if the instructions were different from what we had discussed with God earlier.

The journey to Eden would require a whole lot of grace. Acquire the knowledge, meditate, and act to see His grace at work in your life all the time.

Breeding Empathy and not Contempt!

Before concluding this chapter on grace, I would like to explore one very important sub-topic. As different as we are as human beings, so also are our experiences with God. Individually, we all have areas in our development that we are strong. It could be in areas of giftings or our inability to fall for certain temptations.

Some of us are fantastic musicians. We are good with our voices and instruments while some others wouldn't know a treble clef from a bass clef, it'll be for them like walking with two left legs or knocked knees.

I'd like to focus on a sermon I came across on grace a while ago. I suspect that it was a sermon by Bishop Keith Butler on grace during the West Africa Believers Convention (WAFBEC) 2019. He made a fascinating observation about Paul if you look closer at some of the backing scriptures about his characteristics.

> I came to you in weakness with great
> fear and trembling.
> 1 Corinthians 2:3 (NIV)

> By the humility and gentleness of
> Christ, I appeal to you—I, Paul, who
> am "timid" when face to face with you,
> but "bold" toward you when away!
> 2 Corinthians 10:1 (NIV)

> For some say, "His letters are weighty
> and forceful, but in person he is
> unimpressive and his speaking
> amounts to nothing."
> 2 Corinthians 10:10 (NIV)

These verses paint a general picture of the physical presence of Paul. He wasn't physically intimidating. When he spoke, he appeared to be timid and fearful, not one to inspire confidence in his speaking. He wasn't eloquent or verbose. He wasn't an orator like you would see in the likes of Peter or even Stephen. These men spoke, and many were convicted. Peter recorded 3,000 converts at his first sermon. But what about Paul? Everything he spoke was with such trembling that it was only by the Spirit of God that his words hit the mark.

We could then look at it this way, that speaking was not one of Paul's strong suits. We could say that he didn't have the grace for it. But in his writing, we see so much power. He wrote over half of the New Testament. Even Peter attested to the strength of Paul's books, which some may find difficult to understand (2 Peter 3:16).

Now, here is the point of this. No one Christian is good at everything. While some may struggle with things that are supposedly easy to do, you also may have your weak areas. It's only by the grace of God that our weaknesses are not public knowledge.

As we talk about the grace of God in terms of gifts and talents, we must also explore this grace as it relates to weaknesses or susceptibilities to certain sins. A lot of us didn't lose our taste for certain habits when we became born again. The flesh is still the flesh.

That's why we should be grateful to God that we didn't fall for certain vices as unbelievers. So when you see a believer dealing with alcohol addiction, porn addiction, vulgar language, and so forth, do not be quick to judge. Sympathize with others the same way Christ sympathizes with you. Would we be hard on ourselves as we would be hard on the individual?

That is not to say we should condone sin. But the grace of God on us should provide room for empathy to help others up and put them on their feet. Rather than looking down on them in contempt, feeling like we are better than them without realizing that, but for the grace of God, you are also nothing.

Peter never looked down on Paul because he was a better speaker than Paul. He did recognize that it was the same Spirit at work in Paul that was at work in him also. And there's no doubt that Paul is an excellent writer. No other person in the bible clearly articulates the details of our redemption or expounds on the truths communicated by Jesus, as Paul did in his letters. The book of Romans alone is so vast and deep. It gives raw details about such topics as our redemption, righteousness, and victory over the devil. The insights communicated by Paul in his letters are also practical as he shows step by step how to apply the truth to daily living.

Eventually, he may have become a great speaker with practice having spoken before the emperor of Rome and other high-ranking dignitaries. But his forte was in his writing. His gift made way for the salvation of millions of Christians even to this day.

We are a body, and not everyone would be as gifted as the other when it comes to our responsibilities or as strong as the other when it comes to strengths.

Let us be of help to each other, pulling each other up.

7

Is it Fair to Be Favored?

And Ruth the Moabite said to Naomi, "Let me go to the fields and pick up the leftover grain behind anyone in whose eyes I find favor."

Naomi said to her, "Go ahead, my daughter."

Ruth 2:2 (NIV)

It is the perfect point to talk about favor. The journey to Eden is mysterious. One of those mysteries is how we walk into situations of timely kindness and open arms from people along the way. We encounter goodness from people whom we least expect and in places where favor is unlikely to show up. I say unlikely because, for the most part, our past speaks louder than our current needs.

For many of us, God has called us to places where we are uninvited. We seem to be crashing a party or raining on someone else's parade. He seats us at tables where we remember the words of David echoing in our ears, "He prepares a table before me in the presence of my enemies." And David perfectly understands the blessing of being uninvited.

First, God brought David to a table among the elders in his family and anointed him as king. Imagine not being invited to your coronation? And all had to stand as the young king was fetched from the wilderness. Then he was given a title above all they could ever have hoped to attain.

Then his father sent David to check on his brothers at the front line of the battle. He arrived just in time for the Philistine to begin another round of taunting the Israelites. After an earful of threats by Goliath, David got wind of the reward for solving the problem. But David's brothers were not happy about him exploiting the opportunity. They associated David with the sheep even though his time for the palace had come, wrapped in a chance.

> When Eliab, David's oldest brother,
> heard him speaking with the men, he
> burned with anger at him and asked,
> "Why have you come down here? And
> with whom did you leave those few
> sheep in the wilderness? I know how
> conceited you are and how wicked
> your heart is; you came down only to
> watch the battle."
> 1 Samuel 17:28 (NIV)

But this was his battle. How could they not have invited the champion to his victory? God brought him to this battle even though nobody knew that it was his battle to win. They couldn't see what God had placed in him, especially those who were present at his coronation.

Many people will be upset when doors open for you that you didn't orchestrate and would attempt to keep you where they prepared for you. Meanwhile, God is making something better for you.

Coincidences will take place on the journey to Eden. You will find yourself in positions for which you couldn't have possibly known to pray. Winds would blow, and you'll find your ship sailing for a shore you didn't know but would fulfill everything you ever dreamed.

When Ruth set out to find work, she searched for a place where she would find favor. She wasn't searching for a position with the best kind of work. Ruth was in survival mode. She just needed to get something doing, and an idea came to her mind to go pick up leftovers from the harvest. It wasn't glamorous. It wasn't the best of jobs to do. A high level of thinking wasn't required to do it. No education was needed to start it. She prayed for favor and favor led her to this menial job.

Favor would always guide you to favorable ideas even though they look like opportunities that are beneath you. But never despise humble beginnings.

Favor doesn't always look glamorous. That's why a lot of people miss it when they see it. Ruth was not searching for a rich man to marry. She just needed an entry-level job. Many people would have refused such an opportunity because it won't make them look good in front of their peers.

But I've come to understand something in life that where you start doesn't matter because situations may come up that would require you to start over. That's where the real test of who we are takes place. If you lose everything or fall from a great height, are you willing to start all over from a lowly position?

Ruth was married before then, and, in that society, being married was a big deal even more of a big deal than it is in some African cultures. Being married gave you status, especially if the family you married into was a wealthy one.

It was a patriarchal society which meant that it was men who worked. Female workers were rare. It was men who provided financial security, and the women gave birth to children and took care of the home. So, if a woman loses her husband, her financial security and protection are threatened. Widows are among the vulnerable people of the society.

In such a case, the next best thing for a widow of child-bearing age was to find another husband. If the late husband had an unmarried brother, he was to continue his late brother's name by taking in his late brother's wife and bearing a son. Ruth didn't have that option since her husband and brother in law were dead.

Where does such a woman start? Where does she begin to live her life again in a society that is not favorably disposed to her gender? She had to start from somewhere, and where better to start from than a place where she could find favor?

God's Justice System Explained

Favor by nature is undeserved. You don't orchestrate it. You don't plan for it. You don't even know when it's going to hit you. You're walking down the street and BAM! Someone looks at you and smiles, and suddenly you have a job. Another person looks at you and smiles, and suddenly you have money in your pocket.

The questions now begin: Why her? Why him? This other guy has been working with this company for years, but this young chap with just a year of work experience was able to get the promotion. Why?

What we are demanding is: God, justify yourself!

Why did you bless this person instead of the other?

Why did she get married before her sister?

How come his business took off so quickly while others have found it difficult to start?

God, justify Yourself!

That's not fair!

It's easy to see why people who walk into an open door have so many enemies. The opposition is angry with God, and they take it out on the blessed person. They feel God isn't fair to them. The funny thing is that in most of these cases, other Christians are the ones raising the accusations at God.

They may not necessarily ask God in prayer, but by their countenance around you, you can conclude that they don't like you because you shouldn't be there. They conclude that God's system of justice is faulty and that in God, we find no equity.

It is understandable when you find unbelievers giving a Christian a hard time for being favored by God. But a fellow Christian? That's difficult to understand.

However, God's justice system is what makes Him who He is.

God would not be God if He were an unfair and inequitable judge. God is just. God is fair, and, in His fairness, He attributes to each one of us equal opportunities to experience His favor as we walk on earth.

So, the question is not about whether God is just or not; the real problem is about how He carries out justice.

We begin to understand that God's favor is an intrinsic part of His justice system. It's not mutually exclusive, nor does it operate on a different wavelength from His system.

God favors you because He is just.

But still, God has no favorites (Romans 2:11).

In other words, no single individual or set of individuals has a monopoly on the favor of God. Everyone can experience His goodness, and everyone should experience His favor. It is not an anomaly or a virus in the system.

Favor is not a glitch!

Favor is the norm!

Qualified for Favor?

For God does not show favoritism.
Romans 2:11 (NIV)

Favoritism is a case where you single out someone for good based on a bias. The treatment of this person is usually preferential and unfair to the exclusion of others.

God doesn't do that!

The favor of God is inclusive rather than exclusive. When God shows a person His goodness, He does it because, first, He is fair. If you investigate the life of the favored person objectively, you would see patterns that show why this person deserved it. I know "deserved" is a strong word, and on the face of it, you could say it negates the core of grace, which is grace being undeserved. But I will explain this.

Secondly, when God shows a person favor, He immediately communicates to those around that person and everyone who hears their story that they also can experience what this person has experienced.

That is the point about favor in people's lives that outsiders don't seem to understand and therefore arrive at the conclusion that God is partial and practices favoritism. Anytime you arrive at this conclusion, you exclude yourself from the experience of His favor.

Let's revisit the first point because it doesn't help to start a somewhat controversial conversation and leave it hanging. The story of Ruth is a perfect example of how God favors people, and it also explains why she deserved that treatment.

Ruth had set out to find a place to work where she would find favor. That was her priority. She found the field of Boaz and went to work. She had no tools and no knowledge of harvesting. All she had was her tenacity. She was going to make it work for her and her mother-in-law.

Boaz also happened to be back from Bethlehem, and while greeting his managers, his gaze turned towards the strange woman. Boaz must have been familiar with his workers because he was able to single her out as out of place. Maybe it was the way she picked her harvest. Probably the awkwardness of being unskilled in a task. But somehow, Boaz knew that this woman was not supposed to be here.

> "Who does that young woman belong
> to?"
> Ruth 2:5 NIV

That was the first question of his investigation. Don't be afraid when people ask questions about you. Don't be scared of being investigated. The results of inquiries usually come out in favor of God's people. After Boaz had found out all he needed to know, he called for the young woman. He gave her the job officially, including protection and other benefits.

> At this, she bowed down with her face
> to the ground. She asked him, "Why
> have I found such favor in your eyes
> that you notice me —a foreigner?"
> Boaz replied, "I've been told all about
> what you have done for your mother-
> in-law since the death of your husband

—how you left your father and mother
and your homeland and came to live
with a people you did not know before.
May the Lord **repay** you for what you
have done. May you be **richly
rewarded** by the Lord, the God of
Israel, under whose wings you have
come to take refuge."
Ruth 2:10-12 (NIV) [emphasis mine]

Notice the words in bold. Boaz decided to do what he did because Ruth had shown kindness to her mother-in-law. Everything that happened to Ruth was God repaying and richly rewarding her. No one deserves grace by nature, but Boaz told Ruth that the kindness she's receiving is repayment and a reward. It's like saying she earned it. There must be a way to reconcile these statements. In a previous chapter, How to Access Grace when You Need It, I mentioned a bit about God's reward system and how He rewards diligence.

Many Bible accounts show the favor of God in action, and I'd like us to visit one of those. It gives a perspective to favor on a national scale.

The Israelites did as Moses instructed
and asked the Egyptians for articles of
silver and gold and for clothing. The
Lord had made the Egyptians
favorably disposed toward the people,
and they gave them what they asked
for; so they plundered the Egyptians.
Exodus 12:35-36 (NIV)

This passage is the account of how the Israelites became wealthy at the expense of the Egyptians. In one day, God transferred the whole wealth of the Egyptians to the Israelites. It wasn't about looting the central treasury of the nation. It was a systematic transfer of wealth at the grassroots. Every family gave the wealth of their home to each Israelite who lived in those households as a slave. By the time God finished, the nation of Egypt was bankrupt.

Why would God do such a thing? Why would God choose to favor the Israelites this way? The why lies in their history. About 400 years before this time, a few generations ago, the Israelites arrived on the scene. God saved the nation of Egypt through the wisdom of Joseph, Pharaoh's second in command. Egypt was doing well before Joseph got there. But with Joseph, the economy of Egypt exploded, and it became a trade superpower. If nations are coming to you for food and sustenance, you must be doing something right.

God delivered Egypt through Israel. But a few generations later, the Israelites were converted to slaves, and they were used to build the nation of Egypt. Fast track to the time Israel was delivered, God favored them and transferred the wealth to them because they made that nation, and the wealth belonged to them.

That is the justice of God at work. That is the favor of God.

God's System of Favor

There will be trouble and distress for
every human being who does evil: first
for the Jew, then for the Gentile; but
glory, honor and peace for everyone

who does good: first for the Jew, then
for the Gentile. For God does not
show favoritism.
Romans 2:9-11 (NIV)

It's time to make the distinction between God's system of
favor and individual acts to specific individuals or groups.
In this, we would also clarify the issue of deserving to be
favored.

The above three verses bring clarity to the whole system of
favor. If you do good, you get good and, if you do evil, you
get evil. That follows the principle of sowing and reaping,
which is one of the foundation principles of the kingdom.

We don't deserve the system because when the rewards of
favor get to an individual, it's usually beyond what they
would have ever thought. That is what makes favor so
undeserving. The weight of the reward is generally so
overwhelming.

A gift opens the way
And ushers the giver into the presence
of the great.
Proverbs 18:16 (NIV)

The above passage puts things in perspective. The effect
of favor can be so overwhelming and can change the entire
trajectory of a person's life. But it all begins because of a
gift the person gave.

Many people have gifts but are not serving. Only what we
give brings us before the great. Wasn't that the case with
Joseph?

Favor means being over-rewarded for the little that you did. That is what trips people up. They look at the person and conclude he didn't deserve that kind of reward for the work he did. And that might as well be true. But that is just one person, and he or she is not an exception. God has put a whole system in place to favor His children. No one is excluded from this system unless one excludes himself by accusing God of favoritism.

So, do we deserve the bountiful harvests God brings our way? Admittedly, we don't. Did we earn the system that God put in place for us to experience His beautiful touch? No, we didn't.

However, even though we do not deserve the system and the size of the blessings He brings, we earn a reward because we chose to take the right actions while others didn't.

I believe there's a system in place for the favor of God, and that is the "how." The system is how favor works. As for why some are not favored, could it be that they have not taken the prescribed actions yet? I've also mentioned that some have taken the notion that God is partial and practices favoritism. But there is a reason why some have not experienced God's favor that I'd like us to explore quickly.

Seasons of Favor

There are times when the road to Eden seems like the road to perdition. And I would talk about that in the next chapter. But then there is a time and a season where opportunities are ripe for the taking.

I have seen something else under the
sun:
The race is not to the swift
Or the battle to the strong,
Nor does food come to the wise
Or wealth to the brilliant
Or favor to the learned;
But time and chance happen to them
all.
Ecclesiastes 9:11 (NIV)

No matter how swift, strong, wise, brilliant or learned you are, seasons will come to each one of us in our lifetimes to test our preparedness. Every day is a season to prepare.

You will always have opportunities to learn and increase your speed, strength, wisdom, brilliance, or learning in the off-season. This season is significant too because if we don't take advantage of the off-season, the season of opportunities to advance will go to waste.

But the exciting part of life is that when it comes to favor, everyone has their solar system. That means that in my winter, someone else is experiencing their summer. My autumn could be your spring. But what connects us as individuals is how we relate with one another in our seasons.

When in my spring, do I reach out to encourage and bless the brother in his winter? What about the brother in his winter? Does he reach out to celebrate and praise God for the man who is experiencing his spring? Or does he envy the man who blossoms because his season to arise has come?

If you are yet to experience seasons of opportunities to advance in the call, take heart. Rejoice with those who are in their harvest. Let's not imagine that God has shut up the heavens over us. We will experience His favor. It's as inevitable as the rise of the sun.

8

Drink the Dregs on the Way to Eden

Going a little farther, he fell with his face to
the ground and prayed, "My Father, if it is
possible, may this cup be taken from me. Yet
not as I will, but as you will."

Matthew 26:39 (NIV)

A few years back, I was extremely overweight. Okay, I'm a
bit on the chubby side right now, but that's a story for
another book. Let's stick to the first story. So, where was
I?

A few years back, I was extremely overweight. In a
moment of clarity, I decided to start eating less and
exercising. You know how people find every opportunity
to advise you about something. Still, it never sinks in until
some defining moment?

The defining moment for me was when I sat down at the edge of the bed to lace my shoes, and I began to heave! My belly was such an obstruction! So I knew I had to hit the gym and start living healthy.

The gym was torture! I had to learn to stay away from some foods. I experienced a lot of pain over the next five months—the pain of commitment to new activities and the hurt from depravity from fun but hurting practices. You could call it evil because the feeling was like being thrown into the crucible every day. I never knew exercise was that demanding, especially when you could barely see your toes, much less touch them.

But it was necessary. My body needed the punishment, and Eden demanded that level of commitment. And so, 35lbs later, I was in my mini-Eden and could breathe a whole lot easier.

How does this story fit into this book about a pleasant and beautiful place called Eden?

Are You All In?

That is the question we all must answer as we approach Eden. Are we ready to drink the cup to the dregs? Are we prepared to learn every lesson, take every beating, betrayal, pain, suffering, and failure along the way to Eden? The promised land requires preparation, and these are the tools it uses to whip us into shape.

Jesus for the joy before Him endured the cross. There's no escaping it. He may have died for us not to experience eternal damnation and death. Still, we should look at the pattern of His life and observe how His people went through periods of preparation before obtaining the promise. Then we should ask ourselves an honest question: How can I think of entering my destiny without drinking from the cup?

I had the treadmills and cycles, Jesus had the cup of suffering, are we going to stick to the dream as the going gets tough?

There's a parable about the man who found a pearl and another who found treasure.

> "The kingdom of heaven is like treasure hidden in a field. When a man found it, he hid it again, and then in his joy went and sold all he had and bought that field.
> "Again, the kingdom of heaven is like a merchant looking for fine pearls. When he found one of great value, he went away and sold everything he had and bought it.
> Matthew 13:44-46 (NIV)

In both instances, these men gave everything they had to acquire something of great value. How much are we willing to give in the pursuit of Eden?

The Cup is Not Your End

> This is what your Sovereign Lord says, your God, who defends his people: "See, I have taken out of your hand the cup that made you stagger; from that cup, the goblet of my wrath, you will never drink again.

Isaiah 51:22 (NIV)

Even though we must drink of the cup, it will not be the end of us. Although our suffering may sometimes feel like death and we get to points where we just can't take it anymore, we will not die along the way. God is going to come through.

God didn't design the cup to end us. He designed it to purify and baptize us for Eden. You need to understand that Eden is a protected place.

> After he drove the man out, he placed
> on the east side of the Garden of Eden
> cherubim and a flaming sword flashing
> back and forth to guard the way to the
> tree of life.
> Genesis 3:24 (NIV)

Blood is what opens the gate to Eden. The soldiers spilled Christ's blood. He drank of the cup, and He emptied it. Every journey would require us to drink of cups that reveal everything about us that we need to deal with before we could step into our dreams. In this way, we spill our blood, our sweat, and tears.

Let's go back to the story with which I started. The manufacturers didn't design the gym equipment to kill you. But they can cause enough suffering to make the person give up the search for a better body.

Along the journey to Eden, trials will come our way that reveal our weaknesses and inadequacies. Trials would begin to make us give up the search for Eden. The journey shows us who we are and who we should be to fit into the goal we have in mind. We must fit into the mold for our destiny.

The journey would bring out the pruning shears and force us to let go of everything we don't need for our destination. We want to be better people, but the real lessons of life are not theoretical. We feel the experiences as we learn them.

The Israelites didn't learn everything about God from the law. They learned a lot of lessons from how they suffered when they made mistakes. The lessons from God are practical, and that's why pain is a useful tool. There's nothing as valuable and humbling as a mistake.

Until you understand that the seed must die for it to grow, you'll continue to fight against the adversities and pain instead of going with it. Pain is a part of the process. It doesn't mean there's no joy in the process, but the problem is that joy is a perspective.

Not everything you go through in life would be joyful but count them all joy. You take it as joy. James 1:2 says to count it all joy when you fall into diverse temptations. The temptation itself isn't joyful, but you count it as joy because of where you are going to. You look at the challenges you face in life in the light of your destination.

What's your perspective?

Perplexed?

> But we have this treasure in jars of clay
> to show that this all-surpassing power
> is from God and not from us. We are
> hard pressed on every side, but not

> crushed; perplexed, but not in despair;
> persecuted, but not abandoned; struck
> down, but not destroyed. We always
> carry around in our body the death of
> Jesus, so that the life of Jesus may also
> be revealed in our body.
> 2 Corinthians 4:7-10 (NIV)

The trials we face on the way to Eden prove two fundamental truths. They demonstrate our weakness, and at the same time, they demonstrate His strength. Every time something happens that reveals how weak we are, an opportunity arises to show how strong God is.

We always carry around in our body the death of Jesus; this means that at any given time, crucifixion is taking place in us. We are continually changing and becoming less and less of self so that more and more of God can be made manifest.

When Christ is made manifest in our lives, we must always acknowledge that it is Christ at work and not by our strength. Because every time we take the glory of Christ for ours and try to prove that it is from us and not Christ, our crucifixion deepens. More and more, we would find that we are jars of clay, fragile, and breakable. In the end, the attraction is Christ in us and not us by ourselves.

I'd like to focus on one phrase right now. I understand being hard-pressed, persecuted, and struck down. Those were, in some way, clear on the first reading. But what does it mean to be perplexed? Many times, we are perplexed, but we don't know that we are. Let's go to the boxing ring.

Have you ever noticed a boxer receive a knockout punch falling to the floor but then stands up during the countdown, and instead of going back into the fight, just stands dazed?

On June 1st, 2019, Andy Ruiz Jr. fought Anthony Joshua for the Unified Heavyweight Title of the World. He was the chubby looking underdog compared to the chiseled frame of Anthony Joshua. The odds were against Andy 25-1 [1], and even his trainers didn't believe he would win the fight. Whether or not Anthony underestimated him, we may never know. Still, Andy came into that fight, ready to leave everything in the ring.

Fast forward to the seventh round. The underdog was proving a challenge for the heavyweight champion. Anthony had been knocked to the mat two times. Then in the seventh round alone, Andy knocked Anthony once then about halfway through Andy threw a wicked left-hook that took the champion by surprise. Anthony went down to the mat for the last time that evening. By the time he got up, it was clear the fight was over [2].

That last knockdown didn't leave Anthony unconscious on the mat. He stood up and walked to the corner, then turned around to face the referee. That look on his face, the confusion, the dazzled strange look that you give an opponent who you didn't expect to upset you. That look is the look of perplexity.

It's one thing to be knocked down, and then you get back up to fight again, which was how Andy responded when Anthony knocked him to the mat. It's another to be knocked down, get back up, and end up confused. I can imagine the kind of thoughts that were going through his mind.

Wasn't this meant to be a cakewalk?

This guy is stronger than expected!

Am I not the champ?

I can't believe this!

The Greek word for perplexed is aporéō which means without resource. It describes a hesitant person, filled with doubt, and doesn't know how to proceed on a matter. To be perplexed is a dangerous place to be in for long because if we do not deal with it, the next stage is despair, which means to be without hope.

There are times on the journey when we are perplexed, not knowing what to do, but God is right there providing light so that we do not lose our hope even as we try to figure out what to do.

Understand a Little Bit more about Confession

I find it interesting that Paul was able to admit his weakness.

We are hard-pressed.

We are perplexed.

We are persecuted.

We are struck down.

Your weaknesses are a good thing, and it helps to acknowledge them.

If you're confused, then admit your confusion. If you're in pain, then acknowledge your pain. The problem is that many times we go ahead to confess our desired end without taking time to deal with our current realities.

The goal is to advertise God, and our weaknesses are the most effective platform. I am weak, but He is strong. Let people know the source of the change. If you don't understand your weaknesses, or what the problem is, how do you know what to confess?

A diagnostic approach to dealing with life issues is essential. You don't have money, why? You're always having problems with your wife, why? We need to face the issues and, as much as possible, understand them. Our understanding of our needs draws us to the right scriptures and prescriptions that would deal with the effects of our weaknesses.

For example, a person is always experiencing a lack in his finances. Then he goes ahead to pray and starts to confess that the Lord shall supply all his needs according to His riches in glory (Philippians 4:19). On the face of it, the prayer looks legit. But a closer look at the person's finances shows that the supply is not the problem. He can't control his spending, and it's draining his account.

He takes expensive trips, eats at fancy restaurants, but can't manage significant expenses like school fees, investments, or business opportunities.

I learned something while listening to a sermon by Pastor Poju Oyemade, Senior Pastor of Covenant Christian Center. He mentioned that as Christians, we should not just focus on the scriptures that talk about the promises of

God. But we should also take time to meditate on
scriptures that talk about God's admonishment and
correction and even include them in our confessions.

Confession is not only about focusing on the environment
and trying to correct everything that doesn't agree with
your current state, views, or disposition on some issues. It's
not only about getting things from the environment, but
it's also about correcting faults in us.

> But who can discern their own errors?
> Forgive my hidden faults.
> Keep your servant also from willful
> sins;
> may they not rule over me.
> Then I will be blameless,
> innocent of great transgression.
> Psalms 19:12-13 (NIV)

God seeks to prepare us for our Eden, and in making us
ready, He must restructure us for the goal. There can be no
restructuring if we don't accept that there's a wrong
structure. It's easier to receive healing if we agree there's
sickness.

Perplexity is a Part of the Journey

Some time ago, I received an invitation to be a Youth
Pastor in a local church. I was so excited. The word of God
was alive! There was nothing better. Every time I settled
down to pray and read the Bible, it was so electrifying. I
got confirmation from the word of God for everything.
Miracles happened along the way that made the journey
possible. I got contracts that were unimaginable for me. I
saw money come into my account in one sitting that I had

never seen before. I knew for sure that God was right there with us.

Then the money ran out! It's a difficult place to be where the money runs out! Then I was involved in a car crash close to winter, where the car was a total loss. So, for that season, my family and I had to rely on the public bus system. I have never felt so humbled.

Other things that were so painful took place. My wife worked for people who, at a time when we needed cash the most, decided not to pay her. We went into some debt because of this. At this point, I had started to doubt the call.

Situations hit us so much that I didn't even know my left from my right. I was so dazed that it seemed like I was just surviving. I thought the problem was the confession, so I got some fresh passages and wrote some new confessions thinking that it would lead to an automatic turn-around. But I was even more dazed when mishap after mishap came our way as a family. There was financial trouble and people trouble and the voice in my head that just refused to keep quiet.

At some point, I lost sight of my vision. I didn't know where I was going anymore. I felt maybe all the confirmation was a mistake. I wanted to go back to my country. I thought I had failed. That was the height of my perplexity. Was I deluded into thinking God would call me? Who was I? What were my qualifications? I decided I wasn't going to the church anymore.

My wife was pregnant at the time with our second daughter, and she needed me. At the end of each month, the rent would wink at us while our bank account wailed. I didn't feel like I was in my calling. I was stuck.

The Dregs are Good for You

Perspective is critical when holding the cup of suffering. It's difficult, almost impossible, to see any good in pain, especially those of the intense type; losing a loved one, experiencing assault, betrayals, backstabbing, and all sorts. But something that David said still intrigues me.

> It was good for me to be afflicted
> So that I might learn your decrees.
> Psalms 119:71 (NIV)

I know David doesn't have a monopoly on suffering, but David is one guy who gets it! Troubles pushed David to the very edge of his mind, but God was right there waiting for him. Despite the pain, I knew God was there. Every time I threw in the towel, He caught it and gave it back to me. I was too tired to go to church, but I listened to Bishop T. D. Jakes podcast, the Potter's Touch, and everything I heard spoke to me.

I learned about trusting God and sticking with what He says. I learned about getting back up. I also learned a great deal about mentorship. At that time, I had stopped talking to my senior pastor. Because every time I saw him, he reminded me of my failures. Eventually, I had to reach out to him.

When I had gotten to the lowest point I could go at the time, I prayed to God:

> I'm sorry for how I've been handling
> this period in my life. Do whatever

> You want to do. Whatever I need to
> learn, help me to learn it.

It was as sincere as I could get. I didn't have so many words. I just wanted everything to make sense. I wanted God to be able to trust me with complicated stuff. I wasn't going to wimp out.

I could say that I understood the love of God. Every time I got to the edge, He was always there waiting. He constantly reminded me that He called me from the start.

There were no miracles of the excess nature like at the beginning of the journey. However, there were still those mercies that were ordinary but all the same impactful. They were not spectacular, but they helped us survive. God was just keeping us below the radar, preparing for the light of Eden.

Now that I look back at that period, I'm glad I survived it with my mind intact and my family together.

Would You Still Have Gone Ahead?

That is a question I often think about, especially when I face some profound challenges. Challenges are beautiful in that they allow you to reflect and check yourself and your motives. If trials don't make you think, then the dream you're pursuing is not big enough. Or, perhaps the challenge is not cut too deep.

At this point, I pause to ask myself if the words I write are not too melancholic. I mean, the book is supposed to be about faith, then joy and hope. Eden is beautiful, and the thought of achieving your goals should make your heart warm up.

But my concern is that not many people will tell you the truth about the sowing experience. We see the struggle of the sower as he waters the ground under the intense heat of the sun. How concerned he gets when the rain doesn't come or when it rains so much that the seed lacks sunlight. But do we see the struggle of the seed itself beneath the ground?

I imagine myself being a seed. The thought of becoming a plant and producing fruit would bring me the utmost joy. But how do I deal with the foreboding thoughts that I must die for that dream to come true?

The longer I stay in the ground, the more I feel the pain of my skin shedding, giving way for the life in me to interact with the essence in the environment so that my dream would come true. No one goes into details on what they had to suffer to get to where they are. Could it be that their heart still cringes at the memory of their pain even though they are in Eden? Or, maybe they pity you because they know what you're about to face. They see in your eyes that the very sign of opposition would send you running back to the safety of a dreamless life?

So, we ask ourselves, if we knew what we were going to face on the journey, would we have embarked on it in the first place?

When the bible says to count it all joy (James 1:2), what message do you think God was trying to pass across? Have you ever considered that a lot of the circumstances we will come across on the journey drain joy rather than give it? To count it as joy could also be expressed to mean: make it joyful. Find comfort in an experience that is not supposed to be joyful. If we feel as the environment wants us to, we will never be happy.

That is not to say that the world is full of sadness. It's just to say that circumstances always threaten our joy, and the only way joy stays alive is if you keep it alive. Sometimes it needs mouth-to-mouth or CPR, but you must keep your happiness alive.

I want to give an example. I don't mean to scare you but just to educate you. I'll start with a question: Why do you get married?

For those who are reading this who have been married for at least five years, ask yourself this question? If you knew the things you knew now about your spouse before you got married, would you still have gotten married?

The reason I ask this question about marriage at the five-year mark is that, for most people, this is when you've seen the real person. You begin to ask yourself questions like: should I fight for this? Should I overlook this habit? Is this something I can endure?

Becoming one flesh goes beyond intercourse. It's about becoming one working unit. To achieve that oneness, just like the seed sheds and dies, each party must shed and die. There would be things you didn't do that you have to start doing. There would be things you enjoy doing that you have to start doing moderately.

In some cases, there would be things that you want your partner to start doing, but you're upset that even though they have started doing it, they are not doing it with joy.

So, they wash the dishes, but they do it grudgingly. They do the laundry, but they do it reluctantly. Then your anger shifts from, "I hate that he doesn't like to do the dishes" to "I hate that he doesn't smile when he does the dishes."

It is around the five-year mark that you first come face to face with everything that you hate about each other. The flaws in their character are so obvious, and even mistakes before marriage come to light. It is around this time that you must decide, like the seed, whether the joy set before you is worth enduring the temporary discomfort to make the marriage work.

No matter the amount of prayer and confirmation you got from God or the lack thereof, the adjustment is necessary. Part of the beauty of marriage is that it reveals things about our partners that we didn't know before. And more so, it shows something about us. The question we then ask ourselves is whether we have the level of maturity and discipline to stay focused on the goal.

Let's take this reasoning a bit further. What do you see when you're a guest at a wedding? Now that the scales have fallen off your eyes, what would you see at a wedding? What prayer would you pray for the couple as you see them dance and entertain the guests? What would you think in your mind? "Hey! What on earth are you doing getting married?!"

These things don't apply to just marriage. I used marriage because I know there are still some people who won't back out when it gets uncomfortable. It's not a social contract. But this line of thought applies to everything that is Eden to us.

You want that dream job so badly, but would you have wanted the job if you knew the character of your future boss was so toxic?

You want to start a business, but would you have stayed in employment if you knew you would have to sleep in your car on some nights?

You want to be a dancer, but would you go ahead if you knew that there would be a time that you'll experience a nasty fall that'll cause an injury? Will you go forward with dancing knowing you'll have to spend six months healing with physiotherapy and deal with depression?

There are risks to every dream. Every dream has a "what if" to go along with it. And honestly, we can't know everything that can go wrong, the same way we can't know everything that would go better than we expected. But this is faith.

> "Suppose one of you wants to build a tower. Won't you first sit down and estimate the cost to see if you have enough money to complete it? For if you lay the foundation and are not able to finish it, everyone who sees it will ridicule you, saying, 'This person began to build and wasn't able to finish.'
> Luke 14:28-30 (NIV)

Every dream has a cost, and faith is practical. It's not something that's just in the air. It's not dreamy. On the way to your dream, you'll encounter practical problems that require practical solutions. Faith is taking all those issues that you foresee to God and saying, "these are the costs and risks as far as I can see." God would then assure you that all those things are taken care of. This way, even if some trouble happens that takes you by surprise, you have an assurance in God that the issue is already taken care of. A miracle could happen, supernatural wisdom or intervention or the grace to endure the negative situation would come into play.

If you approach it this way, you won't continue to whine as the Israelites did: always wanting to go back to Egypt at the slightest discomfort.

Reference

1. Davies, G. (2019). Anthony Joshua urged to sack trainer after shock defeat to Andy Ruiz: 'You can't go to uni with third grade teacher'. [online] The Telegraph. Available at: https://www.telegraph.co.uk/boxing/2019/06/0 3/anthony-joshua-urged-sack-trainer-shock-defeat-andy-ruiz-cant/ [Accessed 11 Nov. 2019].
2. Powers, A. (2019). Anthony Joshua STOPPED by Andy Ruiz Jr in one of biggest upsets in boxing history. [online] Express.co.uk. Available at: https://www.express.co.uk/sport/boxing/11351 27/Anthony-Joshua-knocked-out-Andy-Ruiz-Jr-heavyweight-world-champion [Accessed 11 Nov. 2019].

9

Eden is the Journey

*By faith he made his home in the promised
land like a stranger in a foreign country; he
lived in tents, as did Isaac and Jacob, who
were heirs with him of the same promise.*
Hebrews 11:9 (NIV)

Abraham was right there in the Promised Land. He was
living there, and till the third generation, his heirs were
living in the land. Meanwhile, the possession didn't take
place in his time. The Bible says he made his home like a
stranger in a foreign country.

Do you feel like a stranger in a place meant to be your own?

Do you feel like a stranger in your calling?

Does your calling seem like a place of rejection?

Sometimes it does feel that way, and no matter where you
are in your walk with God, I guarantee that you will feel
that way. That feeling that you know you are where you're

supposed to be, but your experience doesn't match your expectations.

Your Journey Through the Promise

God called Abraham to go to a land that He would show him, and Abraham got there. He didn't miss his way. But why didn't Abraham feel fulfilled? Why did he still have to fight, endure rejection, endure the wait, endure the fear?

Many of us find ourselves in positions where the blessing doesn't feel like a blessing. You get a new job, but there is a bad boss. You finally have a boyfriend, but he has some bad habits.

When we talk about the destination, there's something important to point out. There are three aspects to our goal when we talk about Eden.

First, we have the geographical location of Eden. This location could be a state, a country, a person, a thing which we perceive these with our five senses. You see yourself in another country, or on your wedding day. Maybe it's a new job; you're sitting at your desk or the reception right now, or perhaps you just got back from work. You're cradling your child right now. That is what you experience right now, not a confession or a promise. This experience is Eden.

The Bible asks how do we yet hope for what we already have (Romans 8:24)? You're no longer expecting to be at the location if you're already there and, perhaps, if you're not there yet, the hope is still on.

The second destination is the experience of joy in Eden. You must admit that being in the place of your dreams doesn't necessarily mean you're experiencing the joy of it. The present circumstances that exist in your Eden may not be joyful, but it doesn't mean you can't experience joy. It all depends on your focus: is it on the circumstances or the promise of a better experience?

> Consider it pure joy, my brothers and
> sisters, whenever you face trials of
> many kinds, because you know that the
> testing of your faith produces
> perseverance. Let perseverance finish
> its work so that you may be mature
> and complete, not lacking anything.
> James 1:2-4 (NIV)

That leads to the third destination. I wouldn't call this a destination per se, but rather, a group of goals that I'd call mile markers between the first destination and the second. We can call this group of mile markers a "distance" measured in units of time.

You may not yet have arrived at the perfect experience of your location, but it doesn't change the truth that God has you where He needs you to be. Even though the conditions of your Eden don't give you joy, you can derive satisfaction from the promise of it.

Eden Foretold

The reality of Eden is that God has called it into existence. If He could promise you Eden, then it exists. You're not lost.

> As it is written: "I have made you a
> father of many nations." He is our
> father in the sight of God, in whom he
> believed—the God who gives life to
> the dead and calls into being things
> that were not.
> Romans 4:17 (NIV)

The moment you accepted what God pronounced by faith, you stepped into the fulfillment of that word. This truth is what it is right here: the journey and the destination are inseparable. They are a packaged blessing. You cannot experience one without the other.

Everything you go through, both the celebrations and the pain along the way, are all a blessing. You cannot possibly thank Him for the joys without thanking Him for the pains. I know some things that happen along the way may be heinous and devastating. Some may be our fault or some enemy. They may get you to ask God, "why me?"

But don't despair when these things happen. Don't give up hope. No matter how tempting it is to do so. I know how hard it can be. I understand the pain of things not working out.

However, I'll let you in on a little secret.

The Devil Knows Too

I used to find myself being surprised when things go wrong. But I think I've moved past that. When you understand people, you know what to expect from them. I know what to expect from the devil. He always tries to wreck a good thing.

You need to know something about your blessing. God didn't bless you in isolation. Satan was present when John baptized Jesus. He was waiting and ready to receive Jesus in the testing grounds of the wilderness. Satan was there when He taught the scriptures and performed miracles because those miracles involved casting the devil out of people.

The moment God makes a public show of you, you become a marked man. All it took for Job to get into Satan's crosshairs was for God to boast of him. "Have you seen my servant Job?" and then all hell broke loose in the man's life. Things got missing, and people began to die who didn't need to die.

He may not know the ultimate plan or the details of what God is preparing for you. But he knows you are blessed, and something has been spoken over you to fulfill a purpose. How do I know this? Satan knows what it's like to be blessed, and because of his experience, he can recognize blessed people.

> How you have fallen from heaven,
> morning star, son of the dawn!
> You have been cast down to the earth,
> you who once laid low the nations!
> Isaiah 14:12 (NIV)

He couldn't have had a place in heaven and not be blessed. So, he knows the feeling of being blessed. He can recognize people who are experiencing what was an everyday occurrence for him. He knows singing and joy. He knows the anointing and what it is to be ordained. If he is not kept at bay by the grace of God, he knows how to destroy you because Satan knows how he destroyed himself.

You Are a Battlefield

Because Satan knows, he employs every avenue to disrupt you. Your matter is a huge deal to God. Your Eden is a kingdom priority. God has drafted agents on the earth and angels in heaven to make sure they do everything He has appointed them to do to ensure you make it.

The devil's beef is not with you, at least not directly. His grudge is with God. That's his target. But to get to God, he attacks you because you matter to God.

That's right.

You matter to God!

> "Does Job fear God for nothing?"
> Satan replied. "Have you not put a
> hedge around him and his household
> and everything he has? You have
> blessed the work of his hands, so that
> his flocks and herds are spread
> throughout the land. But now stretch
> out your hand and strike everything he
> has, and he will surely curse you to
> your face."
> Job 1:9-11 (NIV)

Satan wants to ridicule God. He desires to show God what a mistake God made in creating man and that humanity is not worth the trouble. He wants to prove that there's no difference between humankind and himself. Come to think of it; there's no redemption plan for the angels, so why should there be one for us? Why is Satan beyond salvage, but we rest in the bosom of God's grace and mercy?

Look at the Job scenario. Job had everything going for him, and Satan said that Job worshipped God just for the stuff God had given him.

Satan intends to prove to God that man cannot be trusted.

God created man and put the man on a pedestal. Look at the words of the psalmist:

> When I consider your heavens,
>   the work of your fingers,
>   the moon and the stars,
>   which you have set in place,
> what is mankind that you are mindful
>   of them,
> human beings that you care for them?
>   Psalm 8:3-4 (NIV)

Do you know how magnificent the sun is? What about the moon? And then the stars? Then the big question: what is a man that God has exalted to such honor that He cares for us even more than these other big items? God is so mindful of us, attentive to every detail of our lives.

> You have made them a little lower than
>   the angels
> and crowned them with glory and
>   honor.
> You made them rulers over the works
>   of your hands;
> you put everything under their feet:
>   all flocks and herds,
>   and the animals of the wild,
>   the birds in the sky,
>   and the fish in the sea,
> all that swim the paths of the seas.

Psalm 8:5-8 (NIV)

Think about it. Angels don't rule over anything. They are more magnificent, powerful, and impressive. Bigger and stronger than a man. If there was anyone to rule over anything, it should have been the angels, starting with the one called Lucifer. But God threw him out for aspiring for more, and humanity gets forgiveness and mercy?

The angels can't fully understand this salvation. They are yet to see the full picture (1 Peter 1:12). But it gets even worse:

> Are not all angels ministering spirits
> sent to serve those who will inherit
> salvation?
> Hebrews 1:14 (NIV)

God created the universe then placed man over all creation. Then He turns to the angels who have been in existence for a far longer time than man and says, "Your new assignment is to serve My children." Even if those words were not to Satan and his fallen angels, you could understand his fury. "So, if I were still there, this would be my new job? Isn't that a demotion? Why should I serve this species that came after me? I've been in the throne room, I've seen God rule, surely I have more experience than this hour old species!"

Now, do you see the picture? We have an enemy with an intense grudge and hatred for God. An enemy who believes rulership, his birthright, has been handed over to a man who never even asked for it. That is why he'll continue to assault you. He has a point to prove.

The Serpent in the Garden

But isn't this Eden, where everything should be rosy and smooth? Why do I have to fight in Eden? Didn't God place me here?

We never heard anything about the serpent until they got into the garden. The truth is that the challenges of Eden are more than the challenges you'll face elsewhere. Imagine a man without aspirations, waltzing through life like it's his dancefloor. He has no trials and no opposition. The devil has him where he wants him.

But give this man a dream, and then all hell breaks loose. Scheming and backstabbing, cheating, and lying, the pressure begins to force the vision out.

A dream brings liberation, an idea frees the mind, and a goal unlocks hope.

The serpent wants to distract you. Satan wants you to think that what God had in mind for you was for your downfall. If he doesn't disrupt the work itself, then he goes after your family. Satan wants to bring you to the point where you say, "It would have been better if I didn't embark on this journey." Like Adam and Eve, he wants to get you kicked out of the garden.

He wants you out!

10

Can You Lose Eden?

*So the Lord God banished him from the
Garden of Eden to work the ground from
which he had been taken.*

Genesis 3:23 (NIV)

Yes, you can.

It's sad.

But, yes, you can.

Is it possible to work so hard, fight so hard, and give so much and still lose?

I'm a bit hesitant about the words I write in this chapter because, as I write, the reality of my Eden dawns on me. Can I lose it all? After the labor, prayer, fasting, and tears?

I know I shouldn't be talking this way, talking about all the things I did and went through to get to where I am. I shouldn't be because the grace of God is what enabled me. But there's something we need to understand about Eden.

Eden requires a price, but you can't buy it. You won't find Eden on the shelf in the stores. It's not on aisle 5! Eden isn't groceries, and it isn't cheap. But as pricy as it may seem, Eden doesn't hang in a museum, where all you can do is visit, take a glance, and admire it. No, no, no. Eden is within reach. Eden is attainable. But how far are you willing to go for Eden?

Adam had it easy, at least the first Adam did. Oh, but the second Adam, He's the real deal!

A Price Paid in Full

> Son though he was, he learned
> obedience from what he suffered.
> Hebrews 5:8 (NIV)

In an earlier chapter, I asked a question: Are you all in? Eden is not a place of half measures. You give in everything you have to offer. You make all the necessary sacrifices because Eden would demand nothing less than your best. Jesus gave everything to be at the right hand of the Father. But the nature of Christ's sacrifice is this: there are things that Christ did so that you won't have to do. However, there are things that Christ did as an example for you to follow. Hard work and giving your all to a God-given cause is one thing that Jesus did as an example. Grace doesn't replace hard work. Hard work is a product of grace.

> No, I strike a blow to my body and
> make it my slave so that after I have
> preached to others, I myself will not be
> disqualified for the prize.

1 Corinthians 9:27 (NIV)

Paul didn't want to lose the prize after going far. He didn't want to miss Eden. So, he poured out his life like a drink offering. There were no half measures with Paul. What is the dream that God has given you? Where is your Eden? Is it a marriage? Is it a job? Is it a business? Is it a ministry? Pour everything into it. These things will not be successful if you choose to cut corners.

The Blood Signature

There is one resource your dream can't do without, and that's You! He chose you for that dream because there's a specific way you see things. There are particular viewpoints and expertise you could bring to the project. Your DNA is required because the assignment is not just a representation of who God is but of who you are. Your works show people who you are.

A Picasso painting is a Picasso because Picasso produced it. His style and influence are so unique that you don't say, "Picasso painted that picture." Instead, you'll say, "that's a Picasso." It takes a unique expertise to authenticate a painting. I looked up the process through which curators certify an art to be genuinely a Picasso. It goes beyond a mere signature because that can fool anyone. But there are hidden ways through which we sign our projects.

According to The RealReal (2015), there are at least four criteria used to appraise a Picasso. These include the consistency of his signature, the print, the edition of the art, and the paper edges. The list could extend to include an examination of brush strokes and other minute details.

However, it's clear what the curators are for: can they find Picasso in the picture to verify that it is a Picasso?

If a great project is being appraised, with what people know about you, would they be able to verify that this project was your project? If you sign a magnificent work, will they confirm that you indeed did the job, or will you be branded a thief for signing something for which you don't have the blood, sweat, and tears to show?

Your signature on a product begins when the work starts and not when the ink of your physical signature dries off. Your name is who you are. God is an expert curator. When He appraises you, He sees beyond what you said you did. God sees your Eden for what it is. He sees when you're late, cut corners, or steal. God sees your process, and He can tell when your method doesn't match the expected outcome.

You can't separate your character from what you do. How you treat your Eden reflects your personality. And when you don't measure up, you could lose Eden.

But, Is Eden Ever Truly Lost?

I ask myself this question sometimes. Are opportunities lost gone for good? Is there no second chance? You look at people in the Bible who lost opportunities and couldn't regain them anymore. Moses didn't go into Canaan, Saul lost the kingdom to David, and Micah lost the chance to have a child. We could go on and on. But we also see the same occurrence in life. People lose job opportunities, marriages, friendships, possessions, and it seems like that's the end for them.

I firmly believe that nothing is ever truly lost. If God could send a second Adam, Jesus, to restore what was lost, I think that nothing is ever truly lost. The opportunity would always re-present itself to you. It may not be in the same form as the first time, but it's coming. The way may be different, but the substance of opportunities is always the same. The focus is to get you to a place where only you can go, to an experience that only you can understand.

For example, you may have your sights on a spouse, thinking that marrying he or she would lead to an inevitable outcome. But do you know that if you pair three different women with one man, there are multiple possible outcomes for their lives as a couple? It doesn't matter what they expected for their lives going in.

What about two women starting in an organization who expect to be managers in five years? The outcome will not be the same for them.

The point is, even if you think you have lost Eden due to a character defect or a mistake, Eden would always present itself again down the line. Eden's anchor is not physical. If Eden is an experience as we put it earlier, then it can be experienced through different forms.

The fact that the first marriage failed doesn't disqualify a person from marriage forever. Being fired from a job shouldn't keep you from looking for a new one. Opportunities would always present themselves to correct whatever character defects or failures there may have been in the past. It may be more challenging to stand than if you had never fallen. The new opportunity may require more work, but it will present itself nonetheless.

The story of David and Bathsheba in 2nd Samuel 11 is a fantastic example. This period was a low point in the reign of David. He remained in the palace when he should have gone to war. As an accountant, for example, there are certain times of the year when you're not allowed by your employer to take your leave days. An example is during January if your accounting period ends in December. It's that period the auditors show up, and all eyes are on the accounts department to tidy up the books. It's something similar that happened to David, the difference being that he took his days off.

> In the spring, at the time when kings
> go off to war, David sent Joab out with
> the king's men and the whole Israelite
> army. They destroyed the Ammonites
> and besieged Rabbah. But David
> remained in Jerusalem.
> 2 Samuel 11:1 (NIV)

It was a time for war, but he stayed back. That was his first mistake. The second happened when he took Bathsheba. Sometimes I wonder how relevant some of the information the Holy Spirit inspired in the Bible is. David had spotted Bathsheba bathing from the roof of the palace, found her appealing, and slept with her. He knew she was married and knew whose wife she was. He probably thought he could get away with it. But this little information was divulged:

> Then David sent messengers to get
> her. She came to him, and he slept with
> her. (Now she was purifying herself
> from her monthly uncleanness.) Then
> she went back home. The woman

conceived and sent word to David,
saying, "I am pregnant."
2 Samuel 11:4-5 (NIV)

He committed the misdeed at the perfect time. A time when he couldn't hide the crime. Have you ever done the wrong thing with precision in timing? I believe Bathsheba was ovulating at the time. It says that she was purifying herself from her monthly uncleanness. At the same time, some versions state that Bathsheba had just finished purifying herself. That means she was ready to conceive right there and then. And David just happened to be there on time. Talk about the perfect crime!

Why dwell on this story? You can hide your bad character, but the perfect opportunity will arise to show itself someday. Some actions which are detrimental to our character may go unnoticed, and the devil is the master of the cover-up.

The same wisdom he provides to sin continues to be in force until the cover-up is complete. He helps to hide your bad character traits until a time when a cover-up no longer serves his purposes.

But God is light in the darkness, and everything hidden would surely come to light. The difference between God and Satan is that God wants to expose you when you're still in obscurity so that you would learn and go on to build a solid character for the future. But Satan is elusive and deceptive.

He shows you the short cuts and how to cover your tracks, all the while building cracks into your foundation. Then the time comes when your falling will be catastrophic. When your failure will affect everything you've built and not just you. Then what used to be so easy to cover-up starts getting complicated until you have nowhere to hide, just like a deer caught in the headlights.

Bathsheba became pregnant, and David unsuccessfully tried to get Uriah, her husband, to sleep with Bathsheba by bringing him home from the war. As a last-ditch effort, he got Uriah killed along with some other men at the battlefront then took Bathsheba to be his wife. If Uriah alone had died, people might have been suspicious. But he put other people in harm's way, destroying multiple innocent families by taking their husbands, fathers, sons, and brothers just to keep up a façade of innocence. As far as David was concerned, this was the perfect cover-up. He was free to take Bathsheba as his wife.

> The Lord sent Nathan to David. When he came to him, he said, "There were two men in a certain town, one rich and the other poor. The rich man had a very large number of sheep and cattle, but the poor man had nothing except one little ewe lamb he had bought. He raised it, and it grew up with him and his children. It shared his food, drank from his cup and even slept in his arms. It was like a daughter to him.
> "Now a traveler came to the rich man, but the rich man refrained from taking one of his own sheep or cattle to prepare a meal for the traveler who had come to him. Instead, he took the ewe lamb that belonged to the poor man and prepared it for the one who had

come to him."
David burned with anger against the
man and said to Nathan, "As surely as
the Lord lives, the man who did this
must die! He must pay for that lamb
four times over, because he did such a
thing and had no pity."
Then Nathan said to David, "You are
the man! This is what the Lord, the
God of Israel, says: 'I anointed you
king over Israel, and I delivered you
from the hand of Saul. I gave your
master's house to you, and your
master's wives into your arms. I gave
you all Israel and Judah. And if all this
had been too little, I would have given
you even more. Why did you despise
the word of the Lord by doing what is
evil in his eyes? You struck down
Uriah the Hittite with the sword and
took his wife to be your own. You
killed him with the sword of the
Ammonites. Now, therefore, the sword
will never depart from your house,
because you despised me and took the
wife of Uriah the Hittite to be your
own.'
"This is what the Lord says: 'Out of
your own household I am going to
bring calamity on you. Before your
very eyes I will take your wives and
give them to one who is close to you,
and he will sleep with your wives in
broad daylight. You did it in secret, but

> I will do this thing in broad daylight
> before all Israel."'
> 2 Samuel 12:1-12 (NIV)

Now, consider this, do you know how long it took for David to admit that what he did was wrong? The whole incident must have lasted at least ten months. But even though no one else knew apart from Joab, God in heaven knew. He sees our cover-ups and exposes them quickly. Through you, God wants to build something magnificent.

We may not know this, but a lot depends on the kind of character we have. It is our character that sustains the blessings that God pours into our lives.

Our character supports the marriage we so desperately wanted.

Our character supports the children we cried for at the altar.

Our character sustains that business opportunity that we stayed up late at night researching.

Now we understand why God was angry with David. God was preparing a foundation for the coming Messiah. God was preparing the lineage for Jesus to come to the earth. He was fashioning out the hidden pathways, and David was threatening to destroy that work by his sin. God couldn't allow that.

Think through your own life. Your Eden is vital to God. When your character doesn't measure up to the demands of the Eden prepared for you, He does one of two things. He either takes Eden away, as He did with King Saul, or

God whips you into shape as He did with David. Rejection or discipline, which would you choose?

God was angry with David, and, according to the word of Nathan, the prophet, the child got sick. God had chosen discipline instead of total rejection. David prayed for mercy that God will spare the child. But the following happened:

> After Nathan had gone home, the Lord struck the child that Uriah's wife had borne to David, and he became ill. David pleaded with God for the child. He fasted and spent the nights lying in sackcloth on the ground. The elders of his household stood beside him to get him up from the ground, but he refused, and he would not eat any food with them.
> On the seventh day the child died. David's attendants were afraid to tell him that the child was dead, for they thought, "While the child was still living, he wouldn't listen to us when we spoke to him. How can we now tell him the child is dead? He may do something desperate."
> David noticed that his attendants were whispering among themselves, and he realized the child was dead. "Is the child dead?" he asked.
> "Yes," they replied, "he is dead."
> Then David got up from the ground. After he had washed, put on lotions and changed his clothes, he went into

the house of the Lord and worshiped.
Then he went to his own house, and at
his request they served him food, and
he ate.
His attendants asked him, "Why are
you acting this way? While the child
was alive, you fasted and wept, but
now that the child is dead, you get up
and eat!"
He answered, "While the child was still
alive, I fasted and wept. I thought,
'Who knows? The Lord may be
gracious to me and let the child live.'
But now that he is dead, why should I
go on fasting? Can I bring him back
again? I will go to him, but he will not
return to me."
Then David comforted his wife
Bathsheba, and he went to her and
made love to her. She gave birth to a
son, and they named him Solomon.
The Lord loved him; and because the
Lord loved him, he sent word through
Nathan the prophet to name him
Jedidiah.
2 Samuel 12:15-25 (NIV)

As far as God was concerned, discipline was His way of showing mercy to David. David lost the child, but he didn't dwell on it. The king cleaned himself up, put on some new clothes and cologne. He ordered some lovely food and refreshed himself. The servants were confused. Shouldn't he be mourning? And honestly, if he were grieving, no one would blame him. Why would they? He was within his emotional right to have a pity party. He could have broken down and stayed down. That's where many of us are. We are so focused on exercising our rights to stay down that we don't realize that we also have a right to rise!

David buried the first child, but Eden presented itself in another form. He rose and had another baby named Solomon, whom God loved and named Jedidiah. If David had stayed down, there would have been no Solomon. The baby he was praying and crying for didn't even have a name! Are you busy crying over some nameless failures that you don't permit yourself to pursue a destiny that would reveal the depth of God's love?

Failure is not the end. Losing doesn't rob you of the right to try again unless you let it. The way I see it, every purpose of God will eventually come to be. Even if failure results in death, God will raise someone to take up the mantle.

Where Terah failed, there was Abraham.

Where Moses failed, there was Joshua.

Where Adam failed, there was Jesus.

The question now is this: after you fall, are you ready to stage a comeback?

Reference

The RealReal, 2015. HOW TO AUTHENTICATE PICASSO ARTWORK. [online] The RealReal. Available at: <https://realstyle.therealreal.com/how-to-authenticate-picasso-artwork-like-an-expert-curator/> [Accessed 24 June 2020].

11

Defending Your Title!

*And from the days of John the Baptist until
the present time, the kingdom of heaven has
endured violent assault, and violent men seize
it by force [as a precious prize—a share in the
heavenly kingdom is sought with most ardent
zeal and intense exertion].*

Matthew 11:12 (AMPC)

Creed versus Drago!

This fight is one of the most exciting I've seen in a movie.
What made it so was not just the match itself but the build-
up, which addressed a crucial question that you must
answer every time you fight for Eden: why?

Why are we in the fight?

From the first installment of the movie, the young Adonis
Creed fought for two things: identity and legacy.

His father was the famous Apollo Creed, and ever since he found out who his father was, he always wanted to live up to that name. Now it's one thing for your heritage to be a secret. In this case, nobody knows who you are or where you're from, and when they relate with you, they treat you like nothing special because they don't expect anything special from you.

That is how God develops you in secret without the interference of people placing demands on you before your time.

However, the moment your heritage is known, people treat you differently. They begin to expect more. Your critics become louder and harsher. Your challengers want to prove they are better than you, not because of what you did but because of the stock from which you were born. They didn't have a chance to defeat your predecessor, but since you bear his name, they might as well challenge the next best thing.

Isn't that why you're so special? The devil couldn't take out God at the beginning and couldn't take out Christ on the cross, and here you are, the next best thing!

> It is enough for students to be like
> their teachers, and servants like their
> masters. If the head of the house has
> been called Beelzebul, how much more
> the members of his household!
> Matthew 10:25 (NIV)

There are some challenges you'll never face unless you are known to be a Christian. People naturally expect something different when they're around you.

Many times you find yourself defending your name, defending your title. Sometimes, it's not just about their expectations, but also their judgment. They judge you for being a Christian based on the failures of someone else they met who didn't live up to the name.

The Devil Plays Dirty!

In Creed 2, Adonis Creed had just won the heavyweight title of the world. He was the world champion. He was hungry and had a lot to prove. Adonis had to prove he was worthy of the title, but not just that, he had to prove that he was worthy of being called a Creed. It was like every challenge he went through was a DNA test.

When he hit the mat the first time: Are you a Creed?

When he took a punch that he should have blocked: Are you a Creed?

When you fall for that temptation: Are you a Christian?

When you didn't speak up for your friend who was oppressed by bullies: Are you a Christian?

When you didn't help that homeless man with a warm meal and hot coffee in winter: Are you a Christian?

We face challenges in life, and every time we go through a problem, we must continuously recheck ourselves. Are we failing the DNA test? Do we measure up to the name we profess to the world?

No sooner had Adonis taken up the title did he face a challenge that was rather savage. The son of the man who killed Apollo Creed, his father, in the ring challenged Creed for the title. Enter Viktor Drago.

As we advance in life, there is a phrase that's whispered across the earth at every level we get to: it is time to unleash Hades. There are opponents for us at each stage of our lives that we cannot advance without facing. But against them, we must stand.

> The gates of Hades will not overcome
> it.
> Matthew 16:18 (NIV)

Some breakthroughs would require you to withstand hell.

That fight broke young Adonis Creed. He endured so many illegal moves from Drago up until the last punch, a deadly right hook as Adonis was kneeling on the mat from his injuries. That was the last straw, and the referee disqualified Drago. Even though Adonis still had the title after the fight and he was still the heavyweight champion of the world, he did not leave that ring a winner. The medics carried him out of the ring, and the next time we see Adonis, he's in the hospital with broken ribs, a ruptured kidney, and several other injuries.

You see, the devil doesn't play nice, and he doesn't follow the rules. The devil plays dirty, and given his way, he'll do everything in his power to prove that we are not worthy just as he isn't. He'll crush you when you are down, and he'll kick you while you're on the ground. Look at the story of Job. The first round of attacks was overkill by any human standards!

> The Lord said to Satan, "Very well,
> then, everything he has is in your
> power, but on the man himself do not
> lay a finger."

Then Satan went out from the
presence of the Lord.

One day when Job's sons and
daughters were feasting and drinking
wine at the oldest brother's house, a
messenger came to Job and said, "The
oxen were plowing and the donkeys
were grazing nearby, and the Sabeans
attacked and made off with them. They
put the servants to the sword, and I am
the only one who has escaped to tell
you!"

While he was still speaking, another
messenger came and said, "The fire of
God fell from the heavens and burned
up the sheep and the servants, and I
am the only one who has escaped to
tell you!"

While he was still speaking, another
messenger came and said, "The
Chaldeans formed three raiding parties
and swept down on your camels and
made off with them. They put the
servants to the sword, and I am the
only one who has escaped to tell you!"

While he was still speaking, yet another
messenger came and said, "Your sons
and daughters were feasting and
drinking wine at the oldest brother's
house, when suddenly a mighty wind
swept in from the desert and struck the
four corners of the house. It collapsed
on them and they are dead, and I am
the only one who has escaped to tell
you!"

Job 1:12-19 (NIV)

Even though Job didn't curse God after this and still maintained his integrity, this kind of tragedy will break any man and bring him to his knees. No matter what type of fire you breathe in the place of prayer, this kind of wound would leave a scar. This kind of pain would cause a dent in your entire belief system. It would leave you stunned and reeling.

I understand you're probably not unfamiliar with hell. You've gone through your share of illegal punches and shots below the belt. You face an enemy that wouldn't hold back—an opponent who wouldn't pull his punches. Thank God for the Referee in the ring because if not, there will be blood.

When the first attack didn't take the title from Job, Satan went for the jugular! He told God that the previous attack was not enough to break Job. He accused God of being unfair and biased towards Job. He accused God of holding back and keeping the boundaries too far out.

He was telling God, "We both know that the attack was just small potatoes compared to my true power! We both know that my attack was not enough to move Job to curse You! Get me in a little bit closer, and I'll show You that Job is not all that!"

Let me take a moment to tell you, my dear reader, that you are stronger than you think you are! The stuff you are made of has its source in God! God vouches for you! The whole of creation is rooting for you!

If Job could survive all that and still stand? Then if you give up on Eden when you lose your job, your friends, your status, a loved one, or anything else that you hold dear, please understand that you gave up too soon. Suicide is not an option, no matter the weight you have to bear. You are stronger than you think, and even Satan knows it. Hear his confession after his attack on Job:

> Then the LORD said to Satan, "Have you considered my servant Job? There is no one on earth like him; he is blameless and upright, a man who fears God and shuns evil. And he still maintains his integrity, though you incited me against him to ruin him without any reason."
> "Skin for skin!" Satan replied. "A man will give all he has for his own life. But now stretch out your hand and strike his flesh and bones, and he will surely curse you to your face."
> Job 2:3-5 (NIV)

Have you ever tried to do something and fail, then when someone questions you about it, you start giving excuses?

You didn't give me enough resources!

You didn't give me enough time!

You didn't give me access!

Reminds us of how Adam blamed God for giving him the imperfect wife. So, just like Adam, Satan blamed God for Job not giving up under attack. And in a way, Satan was right to blame God, because what God has placed in you is beyond human imagination. It's almost like God was cheating and supplying an impossible level of grace behind the scenes as Job went through his trial.

Anytime Satan fails to overcome you, he blames God, and more and more, the devil sees something in you that he doesn't have anymore: God in your corner!

Then the second round of trials came, and Job faced a terrible disease. His blood flowed. It must have been a terrible sight. But look what Job's response was:

> His wife said to him, "Are you still
> maintaining your integrity? Curse God
> and die!"
> He replied, "You are talking like a
> foolish woman. Shall we accept good
> from God, and not trouble?"
> In all this, Job did not sin in what he
> said.
> Job 2:9-10 (NIV)

After this, Satan was mute. We don't hear him in the story of Job anymore.

He wants your title and wants his name called with the greats, but there are rules, kingdom rules, that he will never follow. That's why Satan would forever remain disqualified. But a disqualified fighter has nothing else to lose. Nevertheless, your title remains yours.

The Coach – Fighter Conundrum

Concerning the story of Job, Christians have asked a lot of questions about suffering. And with every new generation of Christians, those questions would always come up. Some would find satisfactory answers, and some won't. But I'll like to explore some aspect of this whole narrative that even I didn't think about until I started talking about Job in the earlier section.

We saw the text, and it says what it says. God expressly agreed to Satan going after Job, and He reduced the circumference of the walls around Job. God ensured that Satan had free reign in his attack on Job to the extent they agreed on. What's done is done.

However, I'd like to explore the relationship between God and Job. What was that like? Let's give Satan a rest for a minute. He did what he did and left the scene. And trust me, the devil will always go. He always flees the scene of the crime. But after a tragedy, two things would forever remain: a loving Father and the broken fighter. That's all Job had left—his relationship with God.

The devil can touch anything in your life, but there is a sacred space he must not cross. You can fight for your relationship with your possessions and people in your life, and that would be admirable. But experience has shown us that we can lose properties and people. However, one thing that is within our control, whether by action or reaction, is our relationship with God, our eternal Father and Life Coach. No one can take that away from you unless you let them.

So, how was Job's relationship with God?

Honest is the first term that comes to mind. Job didn't curse God, and he maintained his integrity. But wow! That man had a mouth on him! There's no doubt that Job could talk about anything and everything with God.

You see, relating to God is not like connecting with people. With people, you can pick and choose what you say while having your real thoughts in your heart. But not with God. Pick and select all you want, but your heart is still laid bare before Him.

I understand some thoughts about God may be so ridiculous that you outrightly reject them. But some things are better off communicated to Him. He may scold you for thinking that way, but I'm very sure that on the face of this planet, since humanity began that people have said worse than you have. He won't hold a grudge against you. If you have questions about your situation, talking plainly to God is better than bottling it in and pretending you don't have doubts. Don't allow bitterness and resentment to take root in your heart towards God.

When Paul faced the thorn in his flesh, he talked to God about it and asked God to get it out. Paul didn't pretend to be over spiritual. He didn't like it, and he told God he didn't. Honesty in communication is one thing that sustains a relationship, and that includes the relationship we have with God.

Now, I'm not advocating for arrogance because honesty and pride are not the same things. You can be honest without being arrogant. You're still God's child.

God Knows Our Secret Fears

Sometimes, when we read the story of Job, we look at the discussion between God and Satan as backstage to what happened to Job.

We are quick to point out that Job didn't know what happened behind the scenes, and if he had been privy to the discussion, maybe he would have "handled" it a little better. Now that I think about it, I think that line of reasoning is flawed on so many levels. There's no "better way" of handling the kind of loss that Job experienced. Knowing that God discussed and agreed with Satan would have made matters worse, in my opinion.

However, have we ever considered that maybe the discussion between God and Satan was the front stage? What if God's relationship with Job was the backdrop of the whole experience? It's worth considering.

Don't follow this reasoning: if Jacob knew about the discussion between God and Satan, he would have done so and so.

Instead, consider this: Did it occur to Satan why God was so quick to agree to his request?

Amid Job's lamentation, we pick up on something that he said. Many well-respected preachers have pointed this out as the key to everything that happened to Job.

> What I feared has come upon me;
> What I dreaded has happened to me.
> Job 3:25 (NIV)

In this statement, we see Job's greatest fear: losing everything. Could this be the backdrop of the whole book of Job? It could be. What happens if you experience your worst fear? Could there be a reason why God continually reminds us not to fear?

In researching this chapter and thinking about Job, it dawned on me that not many people would understand Job just by reading about him. Job is a man you know through experience and not mere knowledge. Until you've been through some deep trials or maybe pursued something and failed, you'll never understand Job's perspective.

The first person that criticized Job was his wife. She told him to curse God and die.

> His wife said to him, "Are you still
> maintaining your integrity? Curse God
> and die!"
> He replied, "You are talking like a
> foolish woman. Shall we accept good
> from God, and not trouble?"
> In all this, Job did not sin in what he
> said.
> Job 2:9-10 (NIV)

Now, in this narrative, it's easy to see her as the villain and as someone trying Job's faith. I mean, "She's tempting him to curse God," and honestly, there are people in life who see you when you fail in pursuing Eden that try to encourage you to give up. I agree that we should not listen to dissenting voices. But I want to shed some light on this woman who was never named.

She lost everything too.

I never realized it until I thought about it. Sometimes in studying the Bible, I now try to adopt a method that I heard Bishop TD Jakes explain. You see, it's easy to focus on the main characters in a bible story because the Bible gives a lot of information about them. But some people are critical to the plot whose emotions and backgrounds are blindsided by the hero's plea that we fail to give them any attention.

Even if we provide them with some notice, it would only be from the hero's perspective. There is little information about them, and we leave their stories to the imagination. But let us try something new. What if you take the time to pull on the thread of those supporting characters? Can we unravel the mystery behind them? Then, you'll have a more exciting plot, and you'll understand their "whys" and correct the wrong categorizations we may have done.

As a man, it's easy to focus on Job. At the time of writing this book, my wife was pregnant with our second child, Zelma, and she's growing fast now, jumping around the house with her elder partner in crime Zoe. So even though I don't feel the pain and discomfort of being pregnant, I can empathize. I see a mother's love and frankly, except there's an anomaly, men can't compete with women in the emotional connection a mother has with their children.

So, when I look at Job's wife, I don't see a villain or foe. I see a wounded mother who lost her ten children at one fell swoop. She is bitter and heartbroken. Lose all the money! Lose all the businesses! Lose all the cows, sheep, and donkeys! Lose all the possessions! But my children?! My children who I nurtured at my breasts, which I carried in my womb for 40 weeks. My children, who I watched helplessly and tried to nurse back to health when they fell ill. I prayed to God, and He brought them back to me. My children who I labored to feed. I can't fully express a mother's love, and honestly, I can't call on my wife, Rachael, to help me put it into words because this chapter would be a book on its own.

I've given you a chance to understand Job's wife that, perhaps, we may vindicate her. We try to absolve ourselves when we fail despite our best intentions. Can we do the same thing for her? Maybe we could also extend the same courtesy to people who have tried to dissuade us from pursuing our dreams?

Could it be that they were hurting from trying to pursue their dreams and failing so much that they became accustomed to failure and gave up trying? Maybe they don't want us to go through what they went through? Perhaps they're angry with us for still trying to hold on to God despite failure, which they couldn't do?

I understand her criticism, and the only thing you can do in such a case is to pursue your Eden and capture it. Maybe that would be their chance at restoration.

This trial was not just about Job. His wife was on trial too!

Never think that when you're in a bond as strong as a marriage that your struggle is not their struggle. Job may have taken center stage, but he wasn't the only one hurting. The book is titled Job, but he wasn't the only one who suffered. They were not the only ones who lost children. There were servants taking care of the animals and all the wealth in the field. The raiders killed people's fathers and sons on account of Job, and the contract was just that of employment.

When we go through suffering, the people closest to us feel it. They may respond to it differently, but they feel it too. So, you may be the center of your world as you see life through your own eyes. But in your peripheral vision, never fail to notice how your suffering affects others too.

I believe that God, asides the conversation with Satan, was trying to teach this couple something. Let's go down memory lane. Think about the trials you've had in your life.

Those tests that made you think, "surely God must come through!" Now ask yourself what your greatest fear was. Or better still think about the area in your life where God is always telling you, "do not fear." For some of us, it's our job and titles. Our status in the community. Our wealth and influence. For others, it's our family and friends. Acceptance from everyone. Sometimes when God says, "do not fear," it's easy to mix up the interpretation. Does He mean, "Do not fear, you're not going to lose it," or, "Do not fear, even though you lose it"?

Don't Be Afraid of Losing

To lend some perspective to Job's experience, let's visit a conversation Jesus had with a young man.

> Just then a man came up to Jesus and asked, "Teacher, what good thing must I do to get eternal life ?"
> "Why do you ask me about what is good?" Jesus replied. "There is only One who is good. If you want to enter life, keep the commandments."
> "Which ones?" he inquired.
> Jesus replied, "'You shall not murder, you shall not commit adultery, you shall not steal, you shall not give false testimony, honor your father and mother,' and 'love your neighbor as yourself.'"
> "All these I have kept," the young man said. "What do I still lack?"
> Jesus answered, "If you want to be perfect, go, sell your possessions and give to the poor, and you will have

treasure in heaven. Then come,
follow me."
When the young man heard this, he
went away sad, because he had great
wealth.
Matthew 19:16-22 (NIV)

There is an important lesson here: if sacrificing something makes you extremely sad, it's what you're most probably afraid of losing.

Don't be afraid of giving up things for God. Because the truth is that what you're so scared to give up willingly will eventually be taken away by force. A lot of the trials we go through are just that. They are about losing things, and we learning to live without those things trusting God to fill in the gap.

If you wanted to summarize the whole book of Job into a phrase, I would put it this way: Is Job committed to God? I think if you look at it from this perspective, the book of Job will make a whole lot of sense.

For many of us, this is the question we should ask ourselves. Would we stay committed to God even though things get awry sometimes? There are some losses that prayer cannot prevent. Sometimes God's focus is on preparing us for the damage rather than preventing us from it.

"Anyone who loves their father or
mother more than me is not worthy of
me; anyone who loves their son or
daughter more than me is not worthy
of me. Whoever does not take up their

> cross and follow me is not worthy of
> me. Whoever finds their life will lose it,
> and whoever loses their life for my
> sake will find it.
> Matthew 10:37-39 (NIV)

The ultimate test of commitment is this: if you lose this thing which you hold most dear, would you still love Me? That is the test the young man failed. Sometimes in walking with God, He just pauses and turns around with His eyes fixed on ours and asks: Why are you following me? Why are you still here?

That was the question Jesus asked the disciples when everyone left Him because of His tough messages. Why are you still here? Our fight for Eden is meaningless unless we can give a meaningful answer to this question. It's a tough road ahead, and if you don't know why you're doing it, challenges will chase you back.

One thing surviving a loss does is that it eliminates the fear of losing. It gives you the boldness to pursue your dreams because "if you could survive that…"

In my previous book, From Seed to Harvest, I talked about losing my job in a restructuring exercise. Though I had many questions, I wouldn't say it was so tight because there was some money involved, and there was still some wiggle room.

The real test was when I got to the United States. With every trial I faced, I kept complaining and wishing I could go back. Challenges struck me on many fronts. We were cheated out of income by people who appeared to be trustworthy. There were times that after paying the bills for the month, all we had left was about $10. Then we had to borrow in some cases or rely on some people's charity.

God had to do a lot of breaking and pruning and teaching so that I let go of who I was to become who He wants me to be.

We learned to ignore our desire for things we didn't need and to wait for stuff we needed but couldn't afford. Like Paul, we learned to live with little and thank God when there was much. Through all of these, we kept telling ourselves that it will all work out. We learned to trust God for things.

As I write this, I realize that in over a year, I never had to see a doctor. Somehow where there was pain or sickness, sleep and some over the counter medication, which I didn't need to depend on for long, solved the problem.

We had to learn to plan expenses with God's direction. Focusing on absolute necessity is a huge thing. For over a year, I wore the same clothes I brought into the country with some additions.

Through all of these, I had to learn to trust God. Meanwhile, did I mention that one of my greatest fears was not being able to provide for my family?

But it got to a point where I was no longer afraid of that. Trust the devil to keep up with the suggestions of failure. But I had been through too much with God. I had one formula for my finances which I strictly followed as best as I could:

- Tithe on everything immediately

- Focus on necessities (but occasionally have a nice $20 meal with my family)
- Save, Save, Save
- Take advantage of every opportunity that comes your way
- Sleep is for lazy people so always choose work before sleep (not so healthy but at this phase it was necessary)
- When you've done all God has shown you to do, leave the unknowns to Him and rest

And when I was honestly doing these, God always took care of the unknowns.

I had to let go of many things. First was my identity. I stopped looking at myself as an accountant or finance professional. When I stripped that away, I saw myself for who I indeed was in God: a very brilliant young man who has a set of skills necessary to solve problems.

In the end, losing things, or as I would instead call it, pruning is a means to an end. You get to show how dependent you are on God. You get to prove your commitment to Him despite all the stuff He has given you. You become more influential in your faith. Right now, I'm at a place in my heart financially that I don't worry about things that would have had me rattled a year ago.

I learn more and more about putting people in their place when it comes to faith. People are people, and God is God. People are resources, while God is the source. Resources may change their mind or decide to do things their way, but God as the Source would never change His mind towards me. I may not always know how, but I know His heart, and I trust Him to fulfill His word.

I'm surprised at my growth, and honestly, if God had shown me how He was going to process and repackage me, I would have told Him, "NO!". But He knows how best to mold you because He made you.

Look at Job in chapter 40 and the Job of chapter 1. The Job in chapter 1 was all together and had everything under control. He purified and made sure his children were right before God. But then he lost all of them. Job in chapters 30 and 31 made some profound statements that it would do you well to read.

At first, Job defended himself before God.

I am no sinner.

I blessed the needy.

I blessed people and showed love to them.

If it was by way of his lifestyle, Job was a perfect man, and he expected only good things to come his way.

> Yet when I hoped for good, evil came;
> when I looked for light, then came
> darkness.
> Job 30:26 (NIV)

He expected good to happen to him based on all that he did and his attitude towards God, but only calamity came to Job. The book of Job, in my opinion, is not a book that contains so many answers. Instead, it highlights the most profound questions in life about good and evil.

Were you molested as a child? Were you raped? Did you lose a loved one? Did you lose your job? Did you get divorced? What about betrayals? What about rejection? Disease? Cancer?

Typically, faith would say make declarations! Speak into your future and reject things that come against your destiny! But there is a wind that blows so unexpectedly that you ask a question that few ever find the right answer to.

Why?

Sovereign God

After Job declared his righteousness and beautiful and kind works as his ticket to a pain-free life, God spoke. Oh, God spoke! I also pondered the words of God in response to Job, and honestly, I had no answer. In all of God's monologue, Job answered twice, and below were his responses to God's questions on wisdom, knowledge, and life.

> Then Job answered the Lord:
> "I am unworthy —how can I reply to you?
> I put my hand over my mouth.
> I spoke once, but I have no answer —
> twice, but I will say no more."
> Job 40:3-5 (NIV)

> Then Job replied to the Lord:
> "I know that you can do all things;
> no purpose of yours can be thwarted.
> You asked, 'Who is this that obscures my plans without knowledge?'

Surely I spoke of things I did not
understand,
things too wonderful for me to know.
"You said, 'Listen now, and I will
speak;
I will question you,
and you shall answer me.'
My ears had heard of you
but now my eyes have seen you.
Therefore I despise myself
and repent in dust and ashes."
Job 42:1-6 (NIV)

If there's one thing to learn from the concluding chapters of Job, it is this: You would have to learn to be satisfied in the journey with some questions going unanswered. Some battles you'll have to fight by faith, and part of it will be not knowing why some things happened the way they did.

God won't answer your every demand for an explanation. Some things you'll just have to accept while trusting in your loving Father. Job came to this point, and you also must come to this point in your journey to Eden. It's the only way you can find healing from the wounds inflicted on the road.

One statement God made to Job stands out to me:

Who has a claim against me that I must
pay?
Everything under heaven belongs to
me.
Job 41:11 (NIV)

12

The Rising Phoenix

*My ears had heard of you but now my eyes
have seen you.*

Job 42:5 (NIV)

The rebuilding process can only begin when you finally surrender to the sovereignty of God because it's only then that you see God and finally experience Him. Your Eden is in God.

God started pulling together the broken pieces of his life to mend them together into something more beautiful when Job surrendered.

Remember the story about Creed and Drago? Adonis Creed had to rise from the bitter loss of the first fight. He had to find his will to fight again. He had to find in himself the reason why he did what he was doing.

First, he dealt with the fear that he wasn't good enough. Dealing with your past concerns sometimes means facing those fears head-on. Just like Job faced his fear of losing everything, Adonis also faced his fear of not being as good as his father. Was he only in the ring because he bore the name? Or, was he in the ring because he was as good as the name?

> Therefore, my brothers and sisters,
> make every effort to confirm your
> calling and election. For if you do these
> things, you will never stumble
> 2 Peter 1:10 (NIV)

The only way you prove your calling is in the ring of opposition. Every time you go to the ring, something dies in you. Trials remove garbage so that you can shine like gold. Like the mythical phoenix, you're reborn after a trial. You're never the same. And even if you failed, it exposes your weaknesses to the light of God. In a way, you're born again. Eden is a place of rebirth.

God is not looking for "name tag" Christians. You see, this is how it works with God. He gives you the title, and then you must prove that you're worth it. The promise tells you that you have the business, but you are going to work it out.

Your failure does not reduce your worth before God, but it does determine what assignments He can entrust to you. If your dad continues to give you the keys to the car after crashing it every time, then he is irresponsible. But God isn't. If you fail, He takes you back into training before He sends you out to try again.

Preparing for Your Comeback

The Adonis, who lost the first fight, wasn't the same one who went in for the second fight. The Adonis who went in for the first fight fought because he was a Creed, he had the heavyweight championship belt, and the whole world was challenging him.

He was on an ego trip. Rocky didn't back him because he knew Adonis wasn't ready for the fight. It's the same way the Israelites tried to enter Canaan after expressing their unbelief; God didn't back the Israelites because they weren't ready.

Sometimes we should be grateful when God doesn't expose us to our dreams too soon. Premature exposure can destroy our destiny. Adonis had to train under Rocky's guidance to face Viktor Drago again. He prepared like never before, and with a full understanding of who he was. He finally understood that a name alone wasn't enough to get him there.

Many of us are searching for Eden. But there is a place of preparation that, if we do not go through, would make us unworthy. We may end up deserting God altogether. However, we must train patiently. The training ground of God is never a place we go through in vain.

In training, God takes your fear away. Creed feared that he wasn't good enough, but, in his brokenness, he dealt with it. Your message to the world comes from your ashes. There's no story to tell without ashes. The ashes are proof that you're reborn. What you left behind to be who you are is a powerful testimony. It's as important as where you're going.

Your past is your ticket to Eden. It is the proof of your rebirth, and when seen in the proper light, it is the most powerful platform from which you can get into Eden.

Give your pain some perspective. Use it as a springboard. On the one hand, don't let it rob you of your future joy. On the other hand, don't let it go to waste.

Jesus's platform was the cross.

Peter's platform was that he denied Jesus.

Paul's platform was that he was the chief among sinners because he persecuted Christians.

Your platform is never attractive. Many people hide their past, and in some cases, it is for a good reason. But the people who make a lasting impact are those who use their history. The cross wasn't attractive, but that is the symbol of Christianity today.

However, we do not worship the cross. No one expects you to praise your pain. No! But we only hope that you do us the goodwill of telling your story right. We worship the Jesus whom God raised from the dead but whose resurrection would have no meaning without the death that led Him there. Just as you would adore the resurrected Christ, celebrate your victory. But remember that your success needs to make sense to the hurting.

People want to escape their pain, so your story needs to answer this question: victory over what?

Coached Through the Pain

There's nothing as important as a guide when navigating unknown territory or finding your footing after a fall. That was the case with Adonis after he had faced Viktor and fallen. During the first fight, he didn't have Rocky in his corner. But who better than Rocky? Rocky had defeated Viktor's father three decades before. He knew how to win. Every so often, on the way to Eden, God would always send some human coaches to be your guide.

Moses had Jethro.

Joshua had Moses.

Samuel had Eli.

David had Samuel, then Nathan.

You can't run in isolation. It matters who is in your corner when you're in the ring.

A coach has many roles, but two things are of importance: he knows where you're going and, more importantly, what you would have to endure to get there. It's good that they cheer you on and give you hope. But the knowledge of what it takes to get there is far more critical than any encouragement you can get. When people train for a marathon, I understand that they practice with a distance that's beyond the official length of the race. What a coach does is assess your tolerance levels for what you would need to endure to get there and train you to increase your tolerance level to surpass that.

Eden isn't a comfortable place. If Eden is a dream job, understand that you must train yourself to keep it because people will try to take it from you. If Eden is a marriage, challenges will threaten it. Every problem we go through in life is in preparation for Eden. And in Eden, experience counts. What training does is to increase your repertoire of resources which you can pull up spontaneously when in the middle of a fight.

There was a significant difference between Adonis's and Viktor's preparation for the rematch. Viktor trained like the fight was going to be a cheap fight. He focused on boosting his confidence. Viktor sparred with partners who couldn't take a punch. He kept knocking them out!

The whole point of preparation is to get to the limit of your capacity and then move on up. Viktor misjudged what he was up against, having never gone past the fourth round in a fight. It is an insult to our problems when we don't prepare well enough for them.

Adonis, on the other hand, was different. Rocky knew what he was up against. His training broke Adonis down. Rocky paired Adonis against people who replayed the power of Viktor Drago in the first fight. He created an environment for Adonis that delivered a semblance of the pain he was going to experience in the ring.

The training was difficult, and some may even call it damaging, but Creed was ready for the fight.

The whole point of the training we go through is that nothing we face in Eden should take us by surprise. If we meet our challenges well, when we get to our destination, any problem we face wouldn't be something new.

No experience we go through is a waste. The challenges we face in life are always preparing us for the next stage, and we all need a human coach who can help put our problems in perspective. The Holy Spirit works through people who, at the time of their challenges, never knew that surviving their pain would be a benefit to you.

Consider the people of Israel. Joshua was the only man who could lead them into the promised Land. He had been groomed by Moses directly, and he was the only one of his generation along with Caleb, who had taken a stand on faith. Joshua had fought in battles that no Israelite alive at the time had, and most importantly, he had seen the promised Land as a spy forty years earlier.

Forty years ago, Joshua had no idea he would be the one to lead the charge against Jericho. He was facing the challenges of his time. But no one told him that, years down the line, others were going to look to him to use everything he learned under the tutelage of Moses for the benefit of the nation.

If you have mentors in your life right now, I can bet that they never had you in mind when they went through their pain.

Whatever you are going through right now is not going to be your end. If you face your troubles manfully, someone is going to benefit from your survival. You will be a source of deliverance in the future if you refuse to give up on your Eden.

Rising through Restoration

The phoenix rises a new bird. From every challenge, we must all rise to be new versions of ourselves. There's nothing you lose on the way to Eden that God wouldn't restore in multiple forms. But restoration is a process that takes time. You must be patient and allow God to work through you. I still find the story of Job fascinating. It's easy to read the book and conclude that the events took about a week. But I believe the story of Job took longer than we think.

We know he lost everything, including his children, in one day. We know he lost his health in one day. Maybe before the end of that week, his friends came, and they had all those conversations which make up the book of Job. But there's this verse towards the end of the book that lends an interesting perspective.

> The Lord blessed the latter part of Job's life more than the former part. He had fourteen thousand sheep, six thousand camels, a thousand yoke of oxen and a thousand donkeys. **And he also had seven sons and three daughters.**
> Job 42:12-13 (NIV) [emphasis mine]

That little phrase adjusts the timeline of the book in my mind. Several things could have happened here. The first is that God could have resurrected Job's original ten children. Knowing God, this is not impossible. But another verse disproves this theory, which is verse 14, where he names his daughters.

I think naming them implies that they were not the original children he had. The second possibility is that his wife could have had all ten children at once. With God, all things are possible, but we must admit that it would be a bit far-fetched. The safe approach, which is the third, is that she had her children over again. By rough estimates, assuming one child per year, Job's restoration to glory took about ten years.

It means that God walked Job through the restoration of his businesses and his empire to a level that was twice what he had. It's not clear how long it took Job to acquire his original wealth. Since his children were old enough to throw parties of their own and make merry, we can assume it took a while to get his initial wealth. And we can assume that his restoration took a shorter time than it took for him to generate the wealth he initially lost.

But let's take a closer look at the process of restoration. As a direct result of Job praying for his friends, first, God turned around Job's fortunes.

> And the Lord turned the captivity of
> Job and restored his fortunes, when he
> prayed for his friends; also the Lord
> gave Job twice as much as he had
> before.
> Job 42:10 (AMPC)

In the King James Version, the first phrase is rendered "And the Lord turned -- the captivity of Job" while the New International Version says, "the Lord restored his fortunes." The first thing God did was to release Job from the advances of Satan. He set Job free. In the same act of release, He restored Job's fortunes. Fortunes, according to the Merriam-Webster dictionary, could mean tangible wealth, or it could mean luck. Coming from God, however, we see favor and grace.

When God turns things around for us, it might not be immediately apparent to others. But eventually, the environment would respond in your favor. The next verses could read as an explanation of how God turned his captivity.

God restored Job's relationships. Everyone who had stayed away came back to him. Job's family and I believe everyone else would include business partners as well.

> All his brothers and sisters and
> everyone who had known him before
> came and ate with him in his house.
> They comforted and consoled him
> over all the trouble the Lord had
> brought on him, and each one gave
> him a piece of silver and a gold ring.
> Job 42:11 (NIV)

I believe God gave Job favor before his old acquaintances. I don't know how many these people were who came back to Job. But what they gave him could have hardly been enough to acquire twice the wealth he formerly had. This little fortune would serve as seed capital for Job, from which he traded and expanded.

When God turns things around for us, it doesn't mean we would lay back and do nothing. It doesn't mean that we would continue to receive and receive from people. We don't acquire wealth through the charity of others. We don't get wealthy out of the pity of others. We produce wealth with God supplying the power and ability (Deuteronomy 8:18). As strong as Job's faith must have been, it means he was also a very diligent man.

We must work hard because God would supply grace in the form of strength and favor before the people we are to meet. We will never rise if we are not ready to work for it. Faith without works is dead. We prove our faith through our actions.

You Can Rise from Anything

Two stories in the bible illustrate this point. Sure, there are more. But I like these stories because they approach setbacks from two perspectives. The first is a setback that is initiated by outside forces, such as the case with Job. Things happen in life that we cannot explain. At those times, we examine our lives. We try to figure out what went wrong, but it just makes no sense to us. Such was the case with Job, and we saw how that played out.

The second story is that of David, which I already covered a few chapters back. David initiated his fall. He went through a lot of trouble as a direct result of what he did. David committed adultery and then murder to cover up the adultery. But he rose from that.

David repented to God even though it took about a year for him to do so. He bore the consequences of his actions gracefully, and he never stopped loving God and singing his praises.

Don't let the mistakes of your past hold you down. Don't let the guilt of having missed it once keep you from having another go at life. We've all missed it at one point or the other in the journey. It is not to say we should have low expectations of ourselves. If we do that, how will we ever improve?

I love how Paul expressed his attitude to life.

Not that I have now attained [this
ideal], or have already been made
perfect, but I press on to lay hold of
(grasp) and make my own, that for
which Christ Jesus (the Messiah) has
laid hold of me and made me His own.
I do not consider, brethren, that I have
captured and made it my own [yet]; but
one thing I do [it is my one aspiration]:
forgetting what lies behind and
straining forward to what lies ahead,
I press on toward the goal to win the
[supreme and heavenly] prize to which
God in Christ Jesus is calling us
upward.
Philippians 3:12-14 (AMPC)

Paul was always forward-looking, no matter the situation.
Whenever he fell, he never allowed it to get to him. But
failure was not an excuse for him to lower the bar on
excellence, especially when it comes to areas of morality
and sin. The world can forgive some inadequacies. They
may frown on it and say there's yet hope for you. Some
attitudes like laziness can be "cured" with a little push, but
one thing people won't tolerate is a moral failure. It would
destroy everything and can decimate in a single hour
everything you built over a lifelong career, whether in
ministry or business.

Honestly, we all have issues we carried over from our sinful
life to our new beginning in Christ. We had a new spirit,
but our body was still the same. The addictions and
attitudes were still there. We were still susceptible to the
same vices under the right amount of pressure.

I've heard of some that miraculously lost the desire for things that used to entice them before. They became Christians, and their bodies lost their taste for alcohol, drugs, pornography, stealing, greed, and whatever else we may identify as sin. It all just went, poof! While for others, it would take time to destroy the strongholds built in their hearts all those years.

As much as we know, we must deal with these issues. But don't let the world hold you down and make you think less of yourself for having giants to fight. The people who judge you harshly for being addicted to drugs probably have some hidden vices eating at them.

True overcomers are the ones who, though firm against sin, are sympathetic to the struggling. They are more likely than not to offer help and not castigate without empathy. It is especially true when you are suffering from the exact thing they overcame.

If you have a drinking habit, seek help from someone who overcame drinking. The overcomer would be firm with you, but you'll never feel unloved.

Jesus doesn't condone sin. But He's touched with the feelings of our infirmities. No matter what your sin is, Jesus is not unapproachable. You'll never feel unloved when you approach God for help.

But social media is a savage place, especially for Christianity. It's devoid of sympathy for anyone who dares to seek help. Christians are making other Christians feel less than nothing because their problems and weaknesses are not the same. The secret drunk accusing the exposed porn addict of being weak because he doesn't know what it's like to face that giant.

Some people have special grace in areas where others struggle. But we must never let others feel less than human because the area of their suffering is unpopular.

Could you imagine what it would have been like if King David faced what he did in this century? Or if Joseph was accused of rape today? Of course, David was guilty, and Joseph wasn't, but eventually, God exposed them for their guilt and innocence, respectively.

The point of all this is not to let exposure keep you from seeking help or moving forward. Paul's attitude was not to let the failures of his past get to him and not to let the successes of his past make him seem more important than he was. Paul always wanted to be better than yesterday. You should do the same.

The truth is that the devil is continually fighting to take Eden from you, and he's not going to stop. He's going to press on. And one of the ways he'll fight you is by trying to expose your weaknesses and your issues to destroy your credibility. People would say, "Physician, heal yourself!"

All dreams involve people. You would work with people to bring a product or service to people. If you're a construction company owner, you're working with people to build a house for another person or set of people. Yes, companies have identities, so you may say, "I'm dealing with the company" or "I'm dealing with the church." Still, all these entities have one thing in common: they are made up of and driven by people.

It matters what people think of you -- not all people, but the right set of people. Some say it doesn't matter what people think, but it does. I know it's a bit grey. But I'll put it this way: work on yourself and strive to be a better Christian than you were.

Some people may not understand you, and that's fine. The only interaction you may ever have with some people will be from your days as an unbeliever. You'll meet people at various stages of your development as a Christian. Some of these people may never have the privilege of seeing the better version of you later in life. The only "you" they may ever meet could be the lazy or hot-tempered you. They'll tell people about that "you," and you may lose opportunities because of who you were. They will judge you and demand apologies for the past life you lived.

When they say those nasty things about you years later, they may be telling the truth based on who you were at the time. Don't hold a grudge against them. It's okay, and it's part of the process.

A time would come that when it matters the most and divine destiny is at its moment. Someone would remember you and speak up for the person that you are right now or would testify to the best version of you that you have developed. Then it won't matter what everyone else thinks. Because when God is ready, He sends the right person that holds the ears and hearts of the right people. My friend, that connection would usher you into Eden. How do I know this?

> When he came to Jerusalem, he tried to
> join the disciples, but they were all
> afraid of him, not believing that he
> really was a disciple. But Barnabas took
> him and brought him to the apostles.
> He told them how Saul on his journey
> had seen the Lord and that the Lord

had spoken to him, and how in
Damascus he had preached fearlessly
in the name of Jesus. So Saul stayed
with them and moved about freely in
Jerusalem, speaking boldly in the name
of the Lord.
Acts 9:26-28 (NIV)

It matters what people think. But even though they think wrongly of you, the time would come when the right person would look on you with favor. He would see in you what others failed to see all along: they focused on the ashes of the old you instead of the glorious phoenix soaring in the skies.

13

Finally...Eden

Instead, they were longing for a better country—a heavenly one. Therefore God is not ashamed to be called their God, for he has prepared a city for them.

Hebrews 11:16 (NIV)

But you have come to Mount Zion, to the city of the living God, the heavenly Jerusalem. You have come to thousands upon thousands of angels in joyful assembly

Hebrews 12:22 (NIV)

My imagination wanders.

I don't know how long you've been on your journey or if you've experienced any breakthroughs recently. But I imagine something happens anytime we meet our targets here on earth. I believe God applauds us. He gives us a series of "well done" and "good job" pats on the back every time we follow through on something.

God would ensure the coming generations hear our legacy of good. We would tell our children, "this is what your life would be like after you have followed God faithfully and walked with Him."

I mean...we call Hebrews 11 the Bible's Hall of Fame. It's a chapter of commendations by God telling the generations to come of those who have pleased Him and whose examples we are to follow.

There is a sense of accomplishment when we achieve things on the earth, and I sincerely believe that God shares in our joy. Of course, the glory belongs to Him for helping us through. There's nothing in the previous chapters that would indicate otherwise. But I believe there's an atmosphere of rejoicing in heaven when any man walks faithfully with God.

Eden is a place of realized expectations. A place of relief and clarity where all our previous suffering makes sense. It's a place where we look ourselves in the mirror and quite literally examine our abs of faith.

I had it in me because of what Christ did for me!

You declare this because the sacrifice of Christ begins to make more sense.

I truly am more than a conqueror!

You exclaim this because until then, you had never really conquered anything on that new level. Now you see the difference between mere confessions when you struggled even to think that the giant you were fighting would fall or what you were working on would ever see the light of day.

You did it! You've reached the summit of your Mount Everest, and God is happy with you. He has always been happy with you.

God's joy is according to what He has placed in you, not necessarily on what you're producing, which may not always be up to par. His rejoicing is in the seed of Christ, which He planted in you.

You did it!

The Big Ask

I'm glad you made it this far!

But I knew you would. Eden is a big deal to you and what better way to equip yourself for the journey than committing to finishing every thing you start?

I want to say thank you once again for completing the book and show you the next steps to take.

Leave a Review

I'd love to know what you thought about the book.

Please leave me a helpful review on Amazon to let me know what you thought and how to make the next version of the book and future releases better.

You could also send me an email at hello@cloakoffire.com to share your thoughts on the book.

~ Olugbenga Ojuroye

Coming 2021

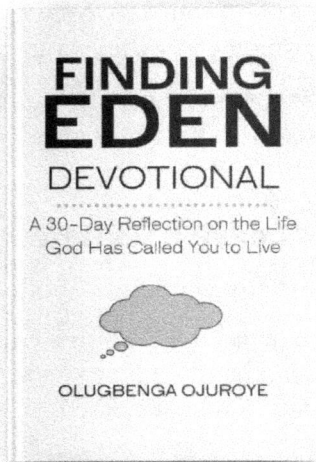

Watch out for *Finding Eden Devotional: A 30-Day Reflection On The Life God Has Called You To Live* in 2021.

If you loved Finding Eden, you would love to read the devotional. It's 30 focused lessons you can read at a 30-Day pace to condition your mind to thrive.

Sign up to get a message when the book is out in stores

https://cloakoffire.com/find-eden-devotional/

About the Author

Olugbenga is a Youth Pastor in New Life City Church, MD, USA. He loves to communicate biblical truth in simple but powerful ways.

Olugbenga loves to write about faith, dealing with trying times, and waiting on God.

You would find Olugbenga's written works on his website, www.cloakoffire.com, and on his Medium Profile, https://medium.com/@Olugbenga.O, where he writes extensively about spirituality in everyday life. He is also the author of From Seed to Harvest, which explores the steps of faith. His goal is to help people live better and more fulfilling lives through his writing.

Olugbenga lives happily with his wife, Imoleayo and daughters, Titobiloluwa and Tiifeoluwa, in Virginia, where they make memories trying out new recipes on the weekends.